*MEDIATION
FOR TROUBLED
MARRIAGES*

MEDIATION FOR TROUBLED MARRIAGES

*Establishing a
Ministry for Conflict
Resolution*

Freya Ottem Hanson

Terje C. Hausken

AUGSBURG • MINNEAPOLIS

*To all families,
especially our own:
My wife, Barbara, and children, Matthew and Katherine
Hausken;
T.H.
My husband, John, and son, John Hanson IV
F.H.*

MEDIATION FOR TROUBLED MARRIAGES
Establishing a Ministry for Conflict Resolution

Copyright © 1989 Augsburg Fortress

All rights reserved. Except for brief quotations in critical articles or reviews, no part of this book may be reproduced in any manner without prior written permission from the publisher. Write to: Permissions, Augsburg Fortress, 426 S. Fifth St., Box 1209, Minneapolis MN 55440.

Scripture quotations unless otherwise noted are from the Holy Bible: New International Version. Copyright 1978 by the New York International Bible Society. Used by permission of Zondervan Bible Publishers.

Cover design: Lecy Design

Library of Congress Cataloging-in-Publication Data

Hanson, Freya Ottem, 1949–
   Mediation for troubled marriages : establishing a ministry for
conflict resolution / Freya Ottem Hanson and Terje C. Hausken.
    p. cm.
   Bibliography: p.
   ISBN 0-8066-2418-3
   1. Divorce mediation—Religious aspects—Christianity.
2. Marriage counseling.   I. Hausken, Terje C., 1947–
II. Title.
BV4012.27.H36   1989
259'.08'655—dc20   89-6534
                                                                              CIP

Manufactured in the U.S.A.   AF 9-2418

1 2 3 4 5 6 7 8 9 0 1 2 3 4 5 6 7 8 9

Contents

Foreword	7
Preface	9
Introduction	11
Part One: The Problem	
1 The Agony of Court Conflict	17
2 The Uses and Misuses of Counseling	35
3 Limitations of Court-ordered Mediation	55
Part Two: A Biblically-based Alternative	
4 Mediation in the Church	71
5 Mediation Is Biblical	94
6 What Happens in Mediation	105
7 Establishing a Ministry of Conflict Resolution	124
Appendix	139
Bibliography	143

Foreword

In the practice of medicine, death is the symbol of failure. Physicians make every effort to preserve life. Consequently, when people are dying, those around them feel the frustration of the situation and may neglect them. A similar situation exists in the church regarding divorce. Divorce is the symbol of failure. All the efforts of the church's ministry, including pastoral counseling, are directed toward reconciling the marriage. As a result, people who are divorcing or who are divorced may feel neglected by their church. They seem to be outside the resources of the church. The pastors and counselors can do little about the divorce settlement. This is turned over to lawyers and the court system.

There is no problem with this in the abstract. Lawyers and judges represent divine callings even as does the clergy, and the legal system is an honorable part of the public sector of God's realm. But the system in our society is so often *adversarial* rather than *mediatorial.* Resources that might be available for reconciliation between persons and for justice for the children are often not realized.

Something is needed between the realization of the marriage's failure and the adversarial system of the divorce courts, and that something is mediation—the subject of this book. Mediation is a resource of the church whose time has come.

Mediation can reconcile the persons even though the marriage is irreconcilable. Reconciliation of the persons can lead to an equitable settlement in a divorce and to decisions made for the welfare of the children.

When people are coerced by the courts, they may do all they can to avoid conforming. The number of husbands, for example, who have not fulfilled the obligations the court has laid upon them, particularly financial obligations, is scandalous. Conformity with the decisions, therefore, is much better when they are mediated rather than decreed through the adversarial system of the courts.

This book charts the ground for a new ministry within the church: mediation for married couples whose marriages, in their estimation, are unsalvageable. Divorce will always be regretted, and even considered a tragedy, but divorce is a reality in our midst. We cannot pretend we have no obligation as a church simply because the couple is not being reconciled as we hoped. It is better to have a fair and decent divorce than a bitter and retaliative experience in the courts. As the book points out, the church's role in mediation is to follow the principle of the apostle: the church ought to settle these matters in its own circles before its members go to the courts (1 Cor. 6:1-6). Once the mediation has been worked out, the court settlement can be on the basis of the good spirit of the mediation decisions.

It is my hope that this book will open the door for this ministry among churches, and that we can make the best out of a bad situation rather than allowing a bad situation to become worse.

WILLIAM E. HULME

Preface

WHY MEDIATION?

Have you noticed how often Christians who are otherwise considerate and helpful can find themselves in destructive, adversarial situations when their marriages run into difficulty? Have you also noticed how often other Christians seem to stand silently by, making statements deploring divorce, but not really knowing what help to offer a couple whose marriage is troubled?

This book is an appeal to individual Christians, the church at large, and professionals in the legal, counseling, and pastoral fields to provide an alternative to the secular, adversarial model of conflict resolution. Mediation is not a cure-all; its purpose is not to save marriages or prevent divorces. But in Christian divorce mediation, the process does include a hope of reconciliation at all stages of the divorcing process, and offers means of conflict resolution that can significantly reduce the bitterness that adversarial settings can foster. And, taking its cue from 1 Corinthians 6:1-6, church mediation also takes seriously the Christian responsibility to engage in peacemaking and mediation before dragging one another into court.

You may find yourself identifying with some of the couples in the case studies. Although they are based on actual situations, information concerning a number of couples has been altered or combined so they will not be identified. Some engaged in complex legal procedures and some in fruitless counseling. They have one thing in common: they are committed Christians who want to live a life of faith and find it difficult to carry on in their own marriages.

This book is born from our experiences as legal and pastoral counselors. We firmly believe Christians need to be actively involved in extending reconciliation and forgiveness to others. Christians need to be involved in peacemaking, since too often we have taken a back seat in this realm.

Mediation for troubled marriages is love interacting in people's lives to bring about forgiveness, hope, and wholeness. Christian mediation for troubled marriages differs from the secular models in one critical way. It acknowledges our human brokenness, our human limitations in the healing ministries, and it humbly and graciously accepts the power of the one, true mediator—Jesus Christ—to transform lives.

Your church may not yet have a mediation program for troubled marriages. Maybe you are the change agent who is called to begin such an effort. Maybe you know someone of vision in your congregation who understands the needs of troubled families and is willing to make mediation a workable possibility. If you are a pastor, you may have been looking for new ways to help families. The program this book describes may be one to consider seriously.

Reconciliation, peacemaking, and mediation are the work of the church.

FREYA OTTEM HANSON
TERJE C. HAUSKEN

Introduction

What is mediation? What are its benefits? Why has mediation become the buzzword of divorce in the latter part of the 20th century? What can mediation do that lawyers in a court of law can't seem to accomplish?

Whether mediation is called family mediation, divorce mediation, or even marriage mediation, the words are synonymous with a process—a process meant to cut the fighting and disputing from the divorce, and to help couples resolve their differences peacefully.

Mediation is designed to help a couple decide their own outcome, instead of leaving those outcomes to counselors, lawyers, and judges. A couple meets with a trained professional mediator who helps the couple decide such issues as spousal maintenance or child support, property divisions, and parental exchange arrangements for the children.

Mediation is often confused with counseling. It is not counseling. Individuals or a couple may rely on a counselor as they try to work through their marital problems. Counseling is often used to help a couple with the day-to-day struggles of a marital relationship so that the marriage will continue. Mediation is uniquely structured to assist the couple in deciding what happens after there is no marriage.

Mediation may also be confused with arbitration. In arbitration settings, disputing parties rely on an arbitrator (who performs the role of a judge) to decide their case for them. In mediation the couple retains the decision-making authority.

Mediation is for those who want to structure their own settlement, and prefer not to leave major decisions up to attorneys and judges.

Mediation may be voluntary, which is the most successful, or it may be court-ordered. Although court-ordered mediation cannot expect the success of mediation that is voluntarily agreed upon, even it has shown positive effects.

Those positive effects have given new hope to couples. Couples who have used mediation in secular settings have seen: positive effects on their children, more honesty, reduced lawyer costs, positive time management, less need to return to court to resolve future problems, increased self-worth during a time when self-esteem usually suffers amazing tolls, and more fairness in the outcome. Although mediation is not always effective, in most cases mediation is a powerful alternative to the traditional agony of the courtroom, and to ongoing counseling when it comes so late that it cannot produce change.

Definitions

Mediation, counseling, arbitration, and court order all are acceptable means of resolving disputes. Mediation differs from the other three in that the parties themselves arrive at an acceptable agreement. That is not necessarily the case in the other three.

Mediation. A process in which parties deal with specific unresolved issues, and, with the aid of a trained mediator, arrive at mutually acceptable agreements which are later formalized in writing.

Counseling. A process in which parties work on unresolved issues, including underlying emotions, on a deeper level, utilizing a counselor for feedback and consultation.

Arbitration. A process in which parties submit to settlement of disputes by the terms set down by an arbitrator.

Court Order. A process in which the parties are ordered by a judge of the judicial system to obey certain terms and conditions.

PART ONE
The Problem

CHAPTER ONE
The Agony of Court Conflict

SANDY AND JOHN

The train ride downtown to the Loop seemed longer than usual. Sandy wasn't thinking about work. It was her 3:00 appointment with the lawyer that occupied her mind. What would her mother think? How disappointed would Grandma be when she learned about the divorce?

Sandy didn't want to hurt any of them, but she was afraid they wouldn't understand. She was Irish Catholic and marriage was for life. Now she was involved in the unthinkable—a divorce. Her mother had been crushed when she had moved out on John to her own apartment. What would Mother say now?

Sandy was pleased there was plenty to do at the office. Her divorce was driving her crazy. "Just help me through this appointment," she prayed. "Help me keep my senses, Lord. I can't hold up much longer."

At 2:30 P.M. Sandy punched her time card and quickly left the building. She looked at the lawyer's address one more time before leaving. Inside the lawyer's office, Sandy told the receptionist who she was and took a seat in the waiting room. One tattered magazine was available, *Parent Magazine*.

Does someone have it in for me? Sandy thought as she paged through the magazine. *I've always wanted one thing in life—to be a mother and wife, and now after seven years of marriage, all I have is a messed up marriage and not even a kid.* Her thoughts were interrupted when her name was called. Sandy ran her fingers through her hair as she walked into the plush corner office. The lawyer cordially greeted Sandy and asked her to sit down.

"Are you here for a divorce?" the lawyer started.

"I just need a lawyer to review some papers for me," Sandy blurted out. "My husband is using a lawyer friend to take care of everything, but I felt I needed someone just to look things over. Do you know what I mean?"

"Are you trying to say there won't be much for me to do?" the lawyer asked.

"There shouldn't be much at all. John said he would take care of everything. His lawyer friend agreed to help him out, but I don't trust him. Besides, he's John's high school buddy. I can't really afford a lawyer."

"I'll try to keep your fees down. Let's just wait until we receive all the papers and then I'll review them for you. Would that be all right?"

"That's fine with me," Sandy responded, breathing a sign of relief.

"Do you know when the papers will be coming?" the attorney asked.

"John told me they were ready. They were just waiting for the address of my attorney. I'll let them know that."

After making arrangements to pay the retainer, which Sandy had saved from her wages, she left the office. She was relieved. She had an attorney, and the whole matter would soon be over.

She had John's assurance that he would take care of everything, that the divorce would be fair, and that she wouldn't have to worry about a thing. Maybe that is what had attracted her to John in the first place. He always appeared so confident, so mature and responsible.

Sandy remembered meeting John when she was a senior in high school. She felt he was an answer to prayer—kind and gentle. The kind of person she wanted for a husband and the father of her children. How anxious they were to get married. She recalled landing the job at Sears, staying at home, and tucking money away for a dream wedding while John finished vocational school. Theirs was a memorable wedding with a high mass, reception, and even a wedding dance. What would those guests think now?

Sandy recalled how badly she wanted a baby. They both agreed to wait. John needed to get his feet on the ground before starting a family—something each of their parents hadn't done. Then John decided to quit the construction job he had and become self-employed. Sandy wondered where that left their plans for a family.

It didn't matter anyway. When they decided to have a baby, she couldn't get pregnant. She counted her infertility a temporary blessing. John was purchasing older houses and fixing them up. They needed her paycheck to cover expenses.

After a year of trying to get pregnant, Sandy convinced John to see a doctor to discuss the problem. John agreed, for Sandy's sake. The doctor couldn't find anything wrong, told them to relax and if she wasn't pregnant within six months to get in touch with an infertility specialist. John refused to seek out other medical help, and Sandy was crushed. She found it hard to look at all the kids in church. The baptisms were the worst.

Her life seemed empty and hopeless, and she couldn't confide in John. He didn't seem to understand. He no longer attended church. He even worked on Sunday on his houses, none of which seemed to get finished. There were tender moments, times when Sandy was convinced this was still a workable marriage; but mostly there were lonely moments, times when Sandy felt isolated from family and church. No one seemed to understand.

Bill collectors started to call. Sandy had signed all the promissory notes and mortgages on the houses. She assured the collectors there would be plenty of money for everyone, as soon as the houses were sold. She started making promises for John. They moved into one of the unfinished houses in order to save money. Sandy cooked in a roughed-in kitchen. Her only running water was from a sink in the bathroom. She started nagging. The quarrels were bitter, and John would often leave for a day or two. His mother took him in and blamed Sandy.

Sandy begged John to consider marriage counseling. He refused and suggested she get help. Sandy arranged for an appointment with her priest. Although he was warm and caring he offered no concrete suggestions for their failing marriage. Sandy returned home confused. She wanted John to see him, too, but John refused.

After six years of marriage, Sandy made an independent decision to move out. She couldn't stand the bill collectors. She couldn't stand living in an unfinished house. Both agreed that a separation might just be what they needed. Sandy found an apartment, but she was scared. She had never lived alone before.

Sandy and John saw each other on occasion over a six-month period. John suggested a divorce.

"I've got a lawyer friend who won't charge much, and he'll take care of all the paperwork for us."

The Agony of Court Conflict

Sandy agreed they needed to do something. She had hoped for a miracle. Since a miracle was not forthcoming, she thought the divorce would at least be friendly. John wouldn't hurt her, after all. But divorce seemed so final.

Sandy thought it over. She was 27—still young. She could find someone else. Why then was John the only one she wanted? Why couldn't someone help them?

After seeing the lawyer, Sandy sensed a finality to her marriage. She felt relief in handing the problem over to an attorney, but it didn't seem to make sense. Divorce was an answer, but it could never seem right.

As she headed to catch the evening train, Sandy suppressed her doubts and worries. Could she trust John to take care of this? He'd made other promises, too, that he wasn't keeping.

The legal papers didn't arrive in her attorney's office as John had promised. Sandy called her attorney weekly to check. There was no communication with John, and she distrusted him more each day.

Sandy was unable to reach John since his phone was disconnected. Days and months went by. She wondered what he was doing. What was his attorney friend doing, anyway? Were the houses getting finished? Had he hired a realtor? Did he sell them without her signature? Did he have a girlfriend? She felt cut off and isolated.

The papers finally arrived—after three months. Sandy's attorney assured her that the divorce could be settled, but it would be best to get the houses marketed so the bills could be paid and the cash assets distributed equally. It appeared that if the three houses sold for fixed-up value, there would be enough money to pay off all the creditors and enough for Sandy to have a modest down-payment on a residence for herself. Sandy was elated to think of a place of her own—a place where landlords weren't king; a place where her cat could live with her instead of with John. That proved to be wishful thinking.

Sandy started making monthly payments on her attorney fees. She soon realized she would need the settlement proceeds to keep up with the lawyer bill. Sandy was getting nervous about the fees.

Sandy drove by the houses just to check, though she was afraid of confronting John. She didn't know how much he had changed. None of the houses had "For Sale" signs on the lawns. Sandy contacted her attorney to inform him. Her lawyer explained that John's attorney wasn't answering any of his correspondence, and his telephone calls were never returned. After the serving of interrogatories (a series of questions) on John's attorney, Sandy felt confident that they would have more information about the amounts owing on the houses and the debts against them, and whether John had found purchasers. John's attorney failed to respond to the document.

"I can bring a legal action to compel a response," Sandy's attorney informed her, "but it will cost money, and it will probably not be heard for four months."

Feeling desperate, Sandy instructed him to go ahead. She felt confident that the court hearing would get John's attention. She heard rumors that the houses were a total mess, and that John was now working for someone else. She didn't know for certain. His mother refused to talk to her or give her any information.

Sandy felt abandoned. She had finally mustered enough strength to tell her own mother, who didn't seem to understand why Sandy had left. After that reaction, Sandy concluded that telling Grandma would have to wait.

Sandy quit attending church. But not taking the Lord's Supper weekly made Sandy feel empty. She told herself it was for the best, but she never felt right with herself or her church. No one from the church called. No one wanted to get involved.

Sandy started going out for drinks after work. Talk was cheap and advice flowed in those establishments. Several barstool experts, veterans of divorce themselves, tried to convince her to change lawyers. "Get yourself a lawyer who can get action on your case," one told her. "Get one that is mean and has an in with the judges," another suggested.

Sandy wasn't unhappy with the lawyer she had, but doubt lingered. Why wasn't he getting this over with?

The court hearing was unsuccessful. John didn't appear, but his lawyer was there. John's attorney couldn't even find his file on John's case. Apparently he had never set one up. The court ordered John to answer the interrogatories within 30 days, or there would be a contempt of court.

The interrogatories were answered within the 30-day period, but they gave little hint as to the status of the property. It came as no surprise to Sandy that none of the houses had been listed for sale, none had been finished, and John had made no payments against the mortgages. What could Sandy do? She had signed all the obligations, and John wasn't paying the debts. "We can make John responsible for the bills in the divorce papers," her attorney informed her, "but the creditors can seek money from you because you signed the notes."

Sandy began to realize the financial mess she was in. Unless the houses were finished and marketed, she might face foreclosure and the loss of any equity she had dreamed of getting out of the divorce.

It was bad enough to have a divorce, but Sandy never dreamed she could also end up in bankruptcy. Finally, Sandy pleaded with her attorney just to end the marriage.

It was already 18 months since the initial filing. Her attorney mailed a settlement agreement to John for his signature. Again, there was no response. "I'll need to schedule this as a contested matter," Sandy's attorney informed her.

"Go ahead and schedule it for contested hearing," Sandy instructed. "It sounds like the only way we are going to get this divorce done."

"There's just one problem," the attorney said. "You already have an unpaid bill here, and I want that paid up before we continue."

Sandy assured him that she would do what she could. That evening she called several other law firms to see if they would handle the case. Each asked if she was presently represented, and none were willing to take her on. "Call legal aid," her coworker friend suggested. Sandy did.

After submitting a financial statement, legal aid determined that Sandy did not qualify. She earned too much money. Sandy felt she would soon be without a lawyer if she didn't come up with a way to pay the balance of the bill. She contacted one of her brothers who refused to give her a loan. Sandy sought out John. Maybe he could help if he understood what was happening to her. She knocked on the door. There was no answer.

After several knocks, John appeared. He looked good. They hadn't seen each other for nearly two years.

"Could we talk?" Sandy asked.

"Sure, come in," John replied.

The house wasn't bad. She saw her cat sitting on a window ledge. Two guys were in the kitchen making supper.

"They pay me rent," John informed her. Sandy pleaded with John to get the divorce resolved. She explained her attorney fee problem and asked how much he was paying.

"We've got a deal," John responded. "I'm doing his kitchen in exchange for the services."

"Is the kitchen done?" asked Sandy.

"Nah, he says I can start whenever."

"Doesn't this whole thing bother you, John?" Sandy asked.

"I've kinda forgotten about it," John answered, but he promised to give his attorney a call in the morning.

John wasn't motivated to do anything. He was living in a house, collecting rent from his roommates and wasn't even paying on the mortgage. He was taking on enough odd jobs to pay for groceries and gas. Although he knew he would eventually lose the house, it didn't seem to bother him. *What's happened to him?* Sandy thought. *What is his future? Is he only existing? Why can't we talk anymore? Why can't someone help us?*

Sandy managed to swing a loan through her credit union. Her attorney filed a contested hearing notice in family court. Thirteen months passed.

It was over three years since their separation when Sandy appeared before the court. John made no appearance, and his attorney made no challenge to Sandy's requests, except that her Sears pension and profit sharing plan be valued and then divided between Sandy and John when she retired or quit work. The court granted the request. There was only one benefit: the divorce was over, and Sandy could start rebuilding her life.

Four months after the divorce, Sandy was served with legal papers from a collection agency. Again, Sandy needed legal representation. Again, her lawyer bills mounted. She was forced to file Chapter 7 bankruptcy in order to save her paycheck. She sold her car to pay the bankruptcy attorney's fees.

Sandy's life was falling apart. She wondered where her family was, and where were those fine church people when she needed them? She wondered where God was, too.

But Sandy's faith in God was deep, and she believed that somehow, some way, God would provide for her. The help she needed came in a person who showed her kindness and love.

Sandy's grandmother called her at work and asked her to stop by after work for supper. Through this dear woman, Sandy began to understand the love of God.

"Sandy, you are welcome to come here for awhile and live," she said. "You can catch the train downtown to your job. I want to help you out. I didn't realize how much you have suffered alone. I wish you had told me sooner."

Through that act of mercy, Sandy started rebuilding her life. She also renewed her trust in a loving and forgiving God.

Sandy returned to her church, but she felt uncomfortable. She joined a nearby Christian fellowship and organized divorce support groups. Sandy wants Christians never to stand silently by again.

Seven years passed after her separation before the houses were sold and the trustee in bankruptcy dispersed the assets and paid creditors. Sandy's life will never be the same—because of the legal struggles she encountered with her own divorce. She is convinced there must be better ways of resolving marital disputes and Christians must be committed to finding them.

THE ADVERSARIAL SYSTEM

The legal system frustrated Sandy. Complex legal language, docket delays, and high costs can leave divorcing couples feeling helpless and victimized.

We're not trying to condemn the legal system in family law matters. Since the mid-1960s, the number of divorce filings per year has tripled. It is amazing that the legal system didn't crumble in the wake of liberalized divorce. Instead, it responded remarkably well. Lawyers, judges, and legislators are to be credited with some of the innovative changes made to meet the demands of families in crisis—families facing divorce.

To elaborate on the laws that have been enacted in the past decade in family law is a subject that deserves more attention than can be given here. Suffice it to say that more humane laws exist because legislatures and courts have responded to the needs of people.

The legal system does work, but it is not an ideal forum in which to resolve disputes if the parties can agree to alternative methods. Even many who work within the adversarial system have welcomed private mediators into the arena of family law. In some states, the courts have mandated mediation for certain family law disputes. For this reason, we believe there are those within the legal system who would also enthusiastically embrace the direct involvement of the church in mediating marital disputes.

In order to understand the benefits of a mediated divorce, it is important to highlight the limitations of adversarial divorce.

Cost

Lawyers cost money. Disputes increase the amount of lawyer time and add to the cost. Often the results don't justify the price tag. Alternatives to adversarial divorce show that when couples can resolve differences, the cost of a divorce is less.

Sandy discovered that paying for an attorney on her salary was financially crippling. No budget is equipped to handle the cost of a divorce, and women in many cases are least capable of handling the cost of hiring an attorney. Although the court may order a husband to pay his wife's attorney fees if she is unable to pay, most attorneys are reluctant to wait. They demand timely payment of fees.

The cost of attorneys "doing battle" has left a bitter taste in the mouths of divorcing couples. Cost is a significant reason for divorcing couples to seek alternative methods in settling marital differences.

Fear

For even the seasoned attorney, the cool, marbled walls of courtrooms can create fear. One of the limitations of adversarial divorce is that it instills a fear of the unknown. There is a fear that someone else is in control. There is a fear of being shamed or of saying the wrong thing, of losing, of looking dumb, or even of being placed in jail.

For the divorcing couple, fear often dictates many decisions. It may instill either a fight or flight mentality. There is a fear of the judge and the laws. There is a fear of legal language and a fear of embarrassment. All of these fears can lead a couple to turn the decision making over to lawyers and judges, and by doing so, the very people who should be making the decisions are not making them. A dependency on third parties emerges.

People are afraid of courts and lawyers. Sandy was afraid of what would happen to her, and her fears are echoed by many others as well. Few people relish the idea of working with a lawyer. Mediation can take some of the fear out of the divorcing process.

Delay

One of the greatest limitations of the judicial system is delays. Delays may be created by the courts, lawyers, or the divorcing couple.

In recent years, one half of all civil court filings have been in the area of family law. Yet our courts and social services have not increased proportionally to accommodate the rapid increase in family law cases. As a result, contested matters may not be heard for final resolution for over a year from the date a contested note of issue is filed with the court. Lives remain unsettled, debts remain unpaid, property depreciates, and hostility may increase during the waiting period.

People need to know where they stand so they can go on with their lives. One judge commented that an early decision is better than a great decision which a couple must wait several months to get.

It took years to conclude Sandy and John's divorce. A significant portion of that time was spent waiting for a court date. However, not all of the delays in the legal system should be blamed on the courts.

Lawyers can also create delays. Failure to promptly respond to correspondence or to return phone calls puts a case on hold. As diligent as a lawyer may be, if the opposing lawyer is uncooperative, delays become inevitable. John's attorney either willfully or neglectfully failed to respond to correspondence. Sandy's attorney had to use costly legal actions to force compliance and get results. There are sensitive, attentive lawyers who are mindful of costs and attempt to reduce delays. But there are also lawyers who create tactical delays and employ expensive, time-consuming information discovery strategies, all of which can serve a good purpose, but which can also create unwarranted delays for an already overstressed couple.

Not all the delays are caused by the courts or the lawyers. The couple can create some delays. Failure to answer the correspondence of an attorney, failure to show at scheduled appointments, failure to let an attorney know of an address change, and failure to comply with an attorney's or the court's request for information, can prolong the divorce procedure.

John didn't show up at two scheduled court hearings. Although his attorney's attendance was adequate in those instances, John's lack of interest in his own divorce created delays that worked a hardship for Sandy.

Mediation, in contrast, can provide for effective time management.

Blame

Adversarial divorce opens many avenues for blame. It's easy for the husband or the wife to point a finger at someone else instead of focusing on creative ways to resolve problems.

Lawyers are often the scapegoats for a divorcing couple. In some instances, the lawyer can be rightly accused for problems that exist. Lawyers can create delays, withhold information, and refuse to work settlements to increase billable hours, but more often blaming a lawyer is only a Band-aid approach to much deeper problems.

Judges also are blamed for unfair decisions or unreasonable delays in making decisions. With a heavy backlog of cases and with increasing numbers of divorce cases being brought before the courts, it is amazing that judges are able to arrive at decisions as quickly as they do.

Social workers are also blamed for unfairness in child-custody cases. One woman complained that the social worker involved in her child-custody investigation only spent one hour with her and didn't interview her witnesses.

Assessing blame distracts from a settlement, makes agreement impossible, and hardens positions. Blame is a side issue but never the real issue, and if too much time is devoted to fault-finding, lives can never be restored, forgiven, and healed. If a friend or neighbor is wrapped up in blaming, it is important to remember that although lawyers, judges, and social workers can be part of the problem, they are not all of the problem. If a change in lawyer, or an appeal or request for a new worker is in order, the wronged party should get on with it, but not spend needless energy complaining about the raw deal he or she is getting. Adversarial divorce seems to be a breeding ground for blame. Mediation is focused on working out future arrangements, not on fault-finding.

Changing laws

To meet public demand, divorce laws have been streamlined and are frequently amended, leaving judges, lawyers, and divorcing couples in confusion. No one seems to have a corner on fairness. No one seems to know what's right. The lack of stability in the law leaves people bewildered. A mediated divorce is less affected by changing laws, and the couple decides what is fair.

Child support

Couples who come to an agreement on an amount of child support are more likely to experience regular and consistent payments than those who have support determined by a court of law.

Clearly, the ongoing collection of child support has emerged as one of the most perplexing issues of this age. In his report to the President, Gary L. Bauer of the U.S. Department of Education stated that 8.7 million women in the United States live with children under age 21 in households where the natural father is absent. Only 58 percent of those women were awarded child support and of those, 80 percent suffer from late payments or no payments at all (*The Family: Preserving America's Future,* December 1986).

Children clearly suffer from lack of child support payments. Adult children of divorce will continue to resent a father who didn't help them out when they were little. Regular and consistent payment of child support is an expression of love.

The Uniform Enforcement of Support Act (the automatic collection of delinquent child support through income tax refunds and paycheck withholdings) are all visible signs of a society that will no longer tolerate the lack of support of children. Even with that act, the legal system can't do everything, and of the child support due, only 70 percent is actually collected annually.

Who suffers? It is clear that women and children suffer from lack of support. In at least 90 percent of the cases, mothers are awarded the custody of minor children and are left to beg social welfare agencies or relatives to support them and their children. After divorce, women, usually without the earning power of their male counterparts, suffer a 73 percent drop in their standard of living. Although divorce laws promote child support and equality of property settlements, it is obvious that even in an age of affirmative action women and children are still the victims.

Visitation

Worse than the failure to pay support is the failure of one of the parents to spend time with their children. In *A Lesser Life: The Myth of Women's Liberation in America,* Sylvia Ann Hewlett cites that in 1987 49 percent of divorced fathers did not see their kids, and the courts were hamstrung to arrive at solutions. Because of disputes with the mother, fathers of children often leave their children starving for a father's love and companionship. Irregular parental exchanges of the children may make sense to a parent who is attempting to rebuild a life, but children don't understand.

John Guidubaldi, professor of psychology in early childhood development, Kent State University, observed that lack of visitation from a father has a far more detrimental effect on boys than on girls. What role model do these young boys have for their own lives as parents? The legal system can't make parents out of folks who don't want to be parents. Who will speak for the children? Do Christians have something to say? There must be more that can be said and done.

Winning

Adversarial divorce supports an "I need to win" mentality. But trying only to win can cloud the real issues. Unlike a personal injury claim, family court is not the place to exercise legal muscle. But often, that is what is done.

Parents may want to "win" a custody battle. A spouse may want to "win" an alimony award, or a large property settlement. The children may be forced to take sides in a custody dispute which alienates the two people they love most. Winning in family court isn't always winning. A public display of private lives may lead to embarrassment, ridicule, hatred, and a desire for revenge that lasts far longer than the moments spent in a courtroom.

The winner attitude in family court creates an ongoing need for lawyers and the courts to resolve problems that are best resolved by the divorcing couple. With court-decided cases, in which one of the spouses did not agree with the decision, lawyers realize that post decree work is a probability.

Full of holes

The legal system functions, but it is flawed. Creative leaders in church and state positions must be open to innovative means of intervening in the crisis facing the family.

As social scientist Amitai Etzioni testified in 1983 before the U.S. Senate Subcommittee on Family and Human Services: "If we continue to dismantle our American family at the accelerating pace we have been doing so since 1965, there will not be a single American family left by the year 2008. While I frankly believe that some force will set in to reverse the course and save the American family before this time, we should not disregard that the trend has been going on for more than a decade and a half."

The legal system is not equipped to save the American family; nor does it claim that saving families is its mission. It often centers its focus on the past instead of providing creative means for couples to restructure their lives after divorce. In many cases, the adversarial system has so prevented the family from reaching any positive outcome that all that remains is isolation, hostility, and revenge.

Where is the love? Where is the forgiveness? Where are the endless possibilities of reconciliation? Is that the mission of the legal system? No, but there must be one or two or three Christians who still believe that love is greater than law, forgiveness greater than hostility, peacemaking greater than warmaking.

Out of the emptiness of the marbled halls of the courthouse, there is a deep need for new help for families. Will the church provide a new resource of strength?

CHAPTER TWO
The Uses and Misuses of Counseling

Don and Ruth

Don sat in the counselor's office staring in disbelief at a woman. She was the woman he had been married to for 25 years—half his life. She wanted a divorce and counseling wasn't going to change her mind. He'd hoped that she would reconsider. He knew he had made mistakes, but she wasn't perfect, either. Wasn't forgiveness in order? Why was she so hard? Why wouldn't she try one more time?

As he turned to look at her again, he reflected on their life—a life masked in the appearance of perfection. Little did his children or members of his parish know the hell they had been living.

Don was a pastor in rural Pennsylvania. His ministry was exceptional. He was a superb preacher. Members of his parish often bragged about their wonderful pastor, asking how long he would stay there before seeking more important positions. Don never missed any meetings dealing with his children whether they were basketball games or teachers' conferences. He took great pride in his children's skills, and his children weren't a disappointment to him.

Beth, an eighth grader, excelled in gymnastics and maintained a straight "A" average. Mark, a senior, was the starting center of the varsity basketball team. He never missed the honor roll. Don's children worked very hard at appearing good.

Ruth, the "ideal" pastor's wife, completed the image of a picture book family. She was active in church activities, a leading soprano in the choir, and an occasional church organist. In addition to her high profile in the church, Ruth was employed by the local high school as an English teacher. She was very strict, but had the complete respect of her students. Ruth also actively participated in civic groups, taking special pride in the garden club she belonged to. She totally transformed the parsonage landscape into a floral fantasy. Ruth was very supportive of her children's athletic and academic endeavors. It could never be said of Ruth that she neglected her duties as a wife and mother!

Don and Ruth worked hard at appearing good. Their days were filled with activity. However, they took precautions to reserve some time alone for themselves and their children. Because of the complicated athletic schedules, this was extremely difficult. But once again, Don and Ruth had to keep up their appearances—even with their children. So 5:00 became the family's time to be together every evening. Ruth would always prepare a wonderful supper. Afterwards, Don would lead the family in devotions. Very often there would be discussions on faith issues and morality. Beth and Mark were so appreciative of both Don and Ruth's openness in dealing with them. They knew they could always turn to their parents when something was bothering them.

After supper, each member of the family would go in his or her own direction. Don usually had meetings or appointments at the church, Ruth would be busy with correcting papers for her English classes, and, if there were no practices held for athletics, Beth and Mark would be occupied with their homework. Don would usually arrive home by 9:30 or 10:00. Ruth would be waiting for him, and they would stay up and watch the evening news together. By 10:30 or 11:00 the whole family would be in bed—except for Don. Don would tell Ruth, "Why don't you go to bed, I'm going to stay up for a while and do some reading. Or I might even go downstairs and work on that chair I've been promising to fix for you."

When Don was sure Ruth was fast asleep, he would make his nightly trip to the basement. He would glance at the chair he had been promising to fix for months, or the unfinished flower box he had been making. Then, he would ceremoniously walk toward his metal storage cabinet where he kept the tools and remove some boxes of nails. With careful precision, he would reach way in the back of the top shelf and produce the prize for a hard day: a bottle of vodka. Of course, to maintain his position in the community, Don thought it best to tell everyone he was a teetotaler. But this was his time to escape into his world of the game he played as a child, "Let's pretend." He would usually drink about one liter of vodka from 11:30 until he went to bed, usually 2:00 or 2:30. Morning would be difficult for Don. Hangovers were regular occurrences. But he would always get up and eat breakfast with the family. After breakfast, Ruth would be the first to leave so she could brace herself for a hard day of teaching. Twenty minutes later, Beth and Mark would leave for school.

Don was never dressed for work by the time they left. He always said it took longer for him to get ready because he wasn't a morning person. When they were gone, he would push himself to get dressed, get in his car, drive around town, wave to a few people, and then go back to the parsonage to sleep off his hangover. He knew that if people saw him in his car, they would think he was out making his daily calls to his parishioners. Don was a true master of this game.

This pattern repeated itself day after day. In fact, this had been his routine for practically 20 years! No one knew. No one suspected—except for Ruth. Oddly, she never confronted him. Occasionally she would prod him about his unfinished projects in the basement. But, remarkably, she never asked about the vodka (though she constantly found empty bottles in the basement, she never attempted to find his hiding place). In effect, Ruth was living in her own world of "Let's pretend."

Life went on as usual for this "exemplary" family until one night. After everyone had gone to bed, Don marched downstairs and repeated his ritual of removing the bottle of vodka from the shelf. He took a few swallows from the bottle, and noticed something peculiar. He was getting drunk on much less booze. This new pattern continued for several months. Again, there was no confrontation from anyone in his family. Things appeared to be "normal." He continued his morning routine, although it was much more work than it had ever been before. Don's greatest frustration came with the "blackouts," when he couldn't remember anything from the night before.

Eventually, the mornings became unbearable for Don. Rather than get up in the morning with his family, he stayed in bed. In fact, he eliminated his entire morning routine from his daily schedule. He started telling stories about having the flu, or being up late, or being called to someone's house in the middle of the night. It wasn't until about noon each day that he eventually began his work schedule. Still no confrontation.

One night after dinner, Ruth and Don were washing the dishes. Ruth asked Don, "Is something wrong? The kids are beginning to ask why their dad isn't around anymore for breakfast. If you're sick, why don't you go to the doctor? Or maybe you're overworked and stressed too much by everything that's going on at church. Maybe you should tell the parish council you're just going to have to cut back."

"Yes," Don said, "that's it. I've been working too much at the church, and I've been so wound up when I get home at night that I just can't seem to get to sleep. So I try to make myself tired by working in the basement or doing some reading."

"Maybe," Ruth said, "you should cut back on your night meetings. They must put you under a lot of stress. Maybe if you didn't have so much stress, then you wouldn't have to—"

"Have to what?" Don asked suspiciously.

"Never mind," Ruth said. "It's been a long day for me. I'm just not making too much sense today. But I've been worrying about you lately. I'm wondering if you get the proper amount of sleep. Why don't you try to cut the meeting short tonight?"

Don started thinking to himself: *She knows. She knows about my late nights in the basement. That's it! I'm going to get rid of the stuff tonight. I can get along without it.*

So that night, after everyone was in bed, Don made his ritualistic trip to the basement. He went with different intentions this time. He reached for his bottle and got ready to dump the contents into the laundry tub. He began to shake. He couldn't do it. He rationalized, "Well, I'll just finish this bottle, and *then* I'll quit."

But the time was never right for Don to quit. There were always the same self-justified excuses: pressures at the church, finances, deadlines, schedules, and so forth. He kept assuring himself, "As soon as I get over this hurdle, I'll quit. I can quit anytime I want. It's just not the right time for me."

One night Don went through his usual drinking routine. In a drunken stupor, he was determined that this was going to be the last time. To prove this to himself—by some drunken logic—he gathered up all the empty bottles (he had hidden over 20 throughout the basement) and threw them in a garbage bag. Then he went to the garage, threw the bag in his car, and took off to dispose of them. He swerved down a country road until he came to an old bridge. He got out of his car, sat on the edge of the bridge, and threw the empty bottles one by one into the water below. He managed, by the grace of God, to make it home that night.

The next morning, Ruth woke Don up and asked, "Don, where on earth is the car?"

The car? Don couldn't remember taking the car out. He managed to get out of bed and look out the window, only to realize that he had parked the car down the street with the right front tire up on the curb. For the first time in years, Ruth did not hide her anger.

"How dare you take the car and jeopardize your life and our reputation! What excuse are you going to give the neighbors? What kind of an excuse are you going to fabricate for me?"

Don was stunned, still trying to remember where he went with the car the night before. He just couldn't understand how he could have been so careless, thoughtless, and foolish as to take the car out when he was totally plastered.

"You can get yourself out of this mess," said Ruth. "I hope you have learned your lesson. Don't think for one minute I don't know what you do every single night!"

"Ruth, I don't know what happened. I ... I ..."

"You were drunk!" Ruth screamed.

There! She said it. After 25 years, Ruth finally mustered enough courage to face reality. Her storybook world had a few cracks in it. And she was finally able to admit that. She felt a sense of loss. But, oddly enough, she also felt a sense of relief.

Don couldn't believe his ears. *Has she known the whole time? Who else knows? Do Beth and Mark have any idea? Is my world falling apart? What's wrong with me? Am I a fraud, a phony? I can't be an alcoholic—can I?*

"Don, you have to do something about this ... this ... this weakness of yours. I can't take the pressure of living like this anymore. I can't stand going to bed at night, crying myself to sleep, knowing what you're doing, and, at the same time, wondering what's going to happen to you. Either you change your way of living or, I promise you, the kids and I will leave."

"Well, what do you want me to do?" Don said meekly.

"Quit drinking. All it takes is a little willpower."

"You're right, Ruth. I will change. Just wait and see, I'll prove to you I'm not an alcoholic. I can quit on my own. Like you say, it only takes a little willpower."

For two weeks, Don's routine totally changed. Instead of staying up until 2:00, he would go to bed with Ruth. But Ruth and the children noticed that Don was not the same anymore. He was tense, nervous, and on edge. He would lose his temper at the most insignificant things. Ruth knew why he was acting like this. But she wanted to protect

Beth and Mark from the "horrible" truth. She explained to them that their father was under severe pressure and stress from the parish board to improve the stewardship program at the church.

That night, Don went to bed when Ruth did. But stayed awake. As soon as he was sure Ruth was asleep, he got out of bed and headed for the basement. Ruth had never asked him where he hid his supply. And just in case, Don kept a spare bottle. He went to the metal cabinet, reached in—it was gone! He started to pace back and forth. What was he going to do? Should he go back to bed? No. He needed a drink. Ruth must have found his hiding place. She was always meddling in his business. She had no business interfering! Don tore up the basement steps, ran into their bedroom, grabbed Ruth by the throat and started shaking her. "Where did you put it? Where is it? Why did you steal it?" he shouted. "You have no business getting into my things. You want me to fail. You want to see me helpless. You can't stand me. You've taken the one thing in my life that can give me comfort."

"Dad! What's going on?" came a voice from the bedroom door. It was Mark. "Dad, what are you doing to Mom?"

"Mark, go back to bed. It's none of your business." Mark lunged at his father, trying to make him release his grip around Ruth's throat.

By this time, Beth heard the commotion, too. She started to cry. Mark, still trying to tear his father away from Ruth, was terrified and confused about what was going on. What was happening to his family?

Don finally fell to his knees, broke down, and cried.

"What's wrong, Dad?" Beth sobbed.

"Beth, I am a sick man. I have just realized that the things that are important to me just don't seem to matter too much anymore because I . . . am . . . an . . . alcoholic."

"Dad," said Mark, "I've known for a long time that you were drinking at night. The other night, after you yelled at me for no reason at all, I figured it was the booze that was doing this to you. I knew where you hid your vodka. It wasn't Mom. I went to your metal cabinet and grabbed the vodka bottle. Dad, do you hear what I'm saying? I was the one who dumped it all out."

Don buried his head in his hands and sobbed. Then he looked at his family and felt a strange sense of relief. Not only did Ruth know, but his children knew as well. Now he could ask for their help.

"I'm going to have to do something about the way I'm treating all of you and myself. I do a lot of counseling in my office. Now it's time for me to take a little of my own advice. I know someone on the parish board who is in AA. Maybe I should take some time and talk with him tomorrow."

"No," Ruth said, still trying to catch her breath. "Call him right now."

"Ruth," Don maintained, "It's after midnight."

"Now!" Ruth said. "You came very close to killing me. Do it now!"

Don hesitantly picked up the phone and called Matthew, a retired farmer from his congregation. Matthew had been sober for about 10 years. His sobriety was largely based on his activity in his local AA chapter. Matthew came over that same night. Don and Matthew talked until 5:00 that morning. Matthew said, "Pastor, you can't stop drinking on your own. You have to have and follow a certain program. You have to remember that alcoholism is a disease, an incurable disease. AA is one option for you. But right now I think you need treatment. Talk it over with Ruth. She will have to be a part of this type of treatment as well."

Don called a meeting of the parish board that next day. He was very surprised to find the support, caring, and understanding that they gave him. In fact, Don was granted a month's leave of absence, with salary, so he could receive the proper treatment.

Don went to a treatment center that was nationally known for its program. He finally realized for the first time in his whole life who he was and why he was an alcoholic. For the first time that Don could ever remember, he could actually live with himself, face himself, and know that he was loved by God! He remained an entire month in treatment. After his fifth step (the last part of the in-patient program), Don was ready to return to his home and church.

There was only one problem. Ruth had been asked to take an active part in Don's recovery, but she hadn't once come to the treatment center! She felt it was his program; he was the one with the disease; he was the one who got himself into this mess in the first place.

Furthermore, it was recommended that Ruth attend Al-Anon, AA's counterpart. Again, she refused to go. "This is Don's problem, not mine," she would say.

While Don progressed in his recovery, Ruth remained in the same frame of mind. She held the same resentments toward Don and the same attitude toward his alcoholism: "Let's pretend there is no problem."

Beth and Mark, on the other hand, were different stories. They became involved in a support group in school for children with alcoholic parents. They were also Don's support while he was in treatment. They realized that alcoholism is a family disease, and that the entire family is sick. They realized that everyone who is an alcoholic family is "recovering," not just the alcoholic.

Don changed a lot over nine months. He began a totally different way of living. He was able to let go of his guilt, hurts, and negative feelings from the past. He also realized he could no longer live a lie—and he didn't have to. He developed a new appreciation of the love of Christ, and how Christ can actively intervene in people's lives.

But Don and Ruth grew further apart. Many times Ruth almost wished Don was back to his old ways. As time went on, Ruth removed herself more and more from Don's job. She maintained a distant relationship with the congregation.

Don feared the congregation the most, and yet it gave him the support he felt he was lacking from his wife. He grew more and more involved in his profession, and unconsciously began withdrawing from his marriage relationship. Because of his program, he had to make AA a way of life. Ruth would have no part in that way of life.

Almost one year to the day after Don's treatment, Ruth announced to Don that she was going to file for a divorce. Don tried hard to convince her this was not the answer. He felt there had to be some way of putting new life and trust back into their marriage. "Ruth, we owe it to ourselves, and to God."

Counseling

The family counselor asked Ruth to state what she felt the reasons were for their failing marriage. Ruth blamed the 25 wasted years of Don's alcohol abuse on his high-pressure job in the church. She further stated that their congregation was responsible for destroying what marriage they had left.

The therapist assigned to Don and Ruth had a good understanding of the disease of alcoholism. She decided the best approach would be to recommend that Ruth and Don receive family counseling in a chemical dependency treatment center.

Efforts to convince Ruth of this totally failed. Ruth made up her mind that counseling was not going to work. She wanted nothing to do with a treatment program. She felt she would be admitting to others and to herself that she was a part of a family illness. Ruth would take no blame. She wasn't the one, after all, who had stayed up until 2:00 in the morning and who had come to bed totally bombed! She wasn't the one who had this "weakness."

No, she thought to herself. *There is no way I'm going to be any part of the blame for Don's problem.*

"It's true," the counselor maintained, "You are not to blame for Don's alcoholism. But his alcoholism has also affected you. Ruth, you have to understand that alcoholism involves the whole family. The only way to treat that illness is to recognize that you have problems, too. You can work on those problems through your participation in a treatment program."

"No," Ruth said. "I am going to proceed with the divorce. As far as I'm concerned, our marriage is over." She got up from her chair and walked out the door.

Don's frustrations began to turn into bitterness and anger toward Ruth. He made a conscious effort to work on his relationships with his children. His greatest fear now was that they would reject him. He wanted them convinced that his love ran very deep for them.

Beth and Mark were devastated by the entire ordeal. They knew their parents had problems. But they couldn't understand the reasons their mom wanted out of the marriage. However, both children were sure of one thing: they loved their parents.

Ruth told her children that she loved Don. But because of his priorities and the misery he had put her through, she could no longer maintain a relationship with him.

"Why do you hate Daddy so much?" asked Beth.

"I don't hate your father, but there are some things that just cannot be changed. We have totally different lives. We have totally different priorities."

"But, Mom, I can't stand to think about us being split up."

"Don't you understand, Beth, that sometimes it's better that a family separate rather than go through constant pain and misery?"

"But, Mom, it seems like you're the only one going through this pain. Dad wants to work things out. Somehow, you can't seem to forgive him. You talk about how terrible he was in the past. But you can't see he's trying to change. Sometimes I get the feeling you don't care about us. You just care about yourself and your own feelings." Beth left the room in tears.

Ruth felt pain and hurt. She knew the kids loved their father. She also knew she did not want to go through unnecessary pain for herself. She thought about how things used to be, and how close knit the whole family seemed to be. Yet during that same time, she had worked hard at covering up Don's alcoholism, even though Don didn't even realize she was aware of his drinking. She thought about her own stress and depression. She thought she was doing the right thing.

Mark removed himself from family life as much as possible. He knew that his parents might put him right in the middle. He had only one more year left of high school, and he was determined that his parents weren't going to wreck his last year. Mark was torn. He actually abhorred the idea of his parents splitting up. To make matters worse, he kept thinking, *If only I would have left that bottle alone, we wouldn't be in this mess now.* Mark couldn't stand the guilt he felt for that discovery.

"Mom," Mark begged one day, "please, please don't divorce Dad. Can't we all try to be the family we once were?"

But Ruth was adamant. After all, she couldn't let her children dictate the future of her marriage. She had to do what she thought was right. One week after Ruth had walked out of the counselor's office for the last time, Don began to make plans to move out. He approached the parish board and explained that he and Ruth were divorcing. He offered to submit his resignation. No questions were asked. The board immediately accepted the resignation.

It was a melancholy day when Don finally left. Don moved his essentials out of the house and loaded them in his car. Beth saw him at the door with his last suitcase. With tears welling up in her eyes, she threw her arms around him and choked out the words, "Dad, just remember that I'm not divorcing you. I . . . love you." And she ran to her room, crying her heart out.

It was Mark who walked his dad to the car. "Dad, I know you needed help, and I know that you are a better person for it. But, Dad, please forgive me for even finding that bottle. Please forgive me for breaking your marriage up." Mark hugged Don, and the tears came.

It was then that Don realized what he needed to say to his son. "Mark, I don't blame you for a bad marriage and a situation that *I* created. I thank you for saving my life. It was because of you that I was able to seek treatment and do something with my life. I am so proud of you and Beth for standing by me through treatment and supporting me in my program. You will always be a part of my life, no matter where I am. I love you, Son."

Don got into his car and as he started driving away, he could see Mark wave to him as he stared through his tears at the father he loved and admired so much. Don felt that part of his life was dying.

Don moved to Pittsburgh where eventually he received another call to serve as an associate pastor of a large church. Ruth remained in the same rural Pennsylvania community, even after moving out of the parsonage.

It was an extremely bitter divorce. Not only did Ruth get custody of the children, but she tried her hardest to limit visitation as much as possible. Don made several efforts to get custody of the children, but he knew that it was a losing battle. Several times he tried to get Ruth to talk to him about visitation. She refused. He could no longer afford the legal expenses to bring the matter back to the court. He would just have to wait for his children to arrive at the legal age when they could make their own decisions.

They tried counseling. But because of the unwillingness of one of the partners, counseling proved ineffective. What more could have been done? What could have helped?

LIMITATIONS OF COUNSELING

Don and Ruth began their counseling when it was already "too late." Usually, the first counsel a couple seeks is from their minister, even when they see little hope. Counselors and clergy know the frustration when that happens. The counselor who worked with Don and Ruth had that experience. Ruth had her mind made up even before their first appointment. There was little the counselor could do.

A man was speaking to his pastor about the divorce proceedings he was going through. "If only we would have come to you earlier! If only we could have seen that our problems were really that *bad!* But now it's too late. There is nothing *you* can do for us. So our only answer is to let the court decide what's best for us." While the man's honesty was commendable, the pastor still didn't know what to say or do for this couple.

While counseling is a tremendous way of solving difficulties in a failing relationship, the fact remains that many couples wait to take this step only as the last resort. Counseling can't work when one of the parties is dead set against it. In looking at the case history of Don and Ruth, we can plainly see that there were many points in their relationship when they could have benefitted from counseling. However, those problems should have been tackled much earlier. As far as Ruth was concerned, by the time they sought counseling, their marriage was over.

After it seems too late

There are several problems from which a marriage seems to have no chance of recovering. The following is a list of some characteristics of deteriorating relationships that can lead to the point of no return.

Infidelity

One of the most talked about reasons for divorce is infidelity. In our day it is commonly known as the "affair." Right away, the one who is having the affair is under scrutiny. It is the pastoral counselor's role, William Hulme writes, to "minister to both partners even when it is only one who is under suspicion of infidelity" (*The Pastoral Care of Families,* Abingdon Press, 1962). Too often the unfaithful partner is not only condemned but shunned by many well-intentioned Christians. This is one reason that "unfaithful" partners do not seek help from the church. It is at this point we should remember that valid Christianity does not try to *create* guilt, but makes every attempt to *remove* it! We should not condone infidelity. There is no question that it is totally contrary to God's purposes in our marriage relationships. However, recognizing that God is our final judge, Christians have no business trying to take over his role. When we do, we close doors; we alienate people. It is the job of the counselor, however, to ask the question, "Why?"

As long as feelings are openly discussed between partners, there is always the encouraging possibility (with a lot of work) that true forgiveness and reconciliation can be the end result.

Alcoholism

Don and Ruth are a good example of this problem. One of the most common signs of our times is chemical dependency. Statistics vary from one in five to one in ten people being an alcoholic. This disease is one of our nation's top killers and is destructive to the home and family.

Needless to say, alcoholism has succeeded in breaking up countless marriages. Connie and Joel had been married for 15 years. Joel had a successful business. Connie helped him in his work as well. There was one problem: Joel was an alcoholic.

Without going into detail, Joel had gone in for treatment four times. His longest period of sobriety was three months.

Eventually Joel lost his business, and Connie eventually divorced him. Unfortunately, this is a common story.

However, as in the case of Don and Ruth, it has also happened that successful sobriety can lead to marital breakdowns. What happened with Don and Ruth? Why would a step in a positive direction eventually lead to a breakdown in the marriage? Since chemical dependency is seen as a disease of the personality, professional treatment deals specifically with the personality. Often the person is literally a changed person. The spouse will see that he or she no longer knows that sober "new" person, and discovers that they can no longer live together. Again, this is a common story.

When the pastor is counselor, he or she is seen as speaking on behalf of the church. As Christians, we can no longer close our eyes to chemical dependency. We, first of all, have to educate ourselves and take a bold look at this disease. Then we have to try to deal with this serious issue.

The pastor can play an active role here. If there is a separation or a crisis in a marriage, the pastor should help identify the problems, including possible chemical dependency. Then he or she can explore the alternatives with the hope of saving the marriage.

Money

One of the most common characteristics of a failing marriage that a counselor can note is a problem with money. This appears more than any of the other characteristics. This one often overlaps the others. The oft-quoted verse, "the love of money is a root of all kinds of evil," can certainly be attested by countless people who have undergone stressful situations because of money. This does not imply that there is necessarily a lack of money. It may be a lack of understanding where each person has his or her priorities with money. It may be a lack of understanding about who has control of the money. Many couples can attest to the fact that there have been many marital arguments regarding this common "evil." Some disputes are carried much further.

Bill and Karen were married for almost 20 years. Bill had a secure job that placed him comfortably in a middle income bracket. But Bill felt a little restless in his job. He didn't like the idea of having to answer to someone else. He wanted to be his own boss, so he pursued the idea of going into business for himself. Karen was opposed to the idea. In fact, she couldn't believe the stupidity of Bill taking such a risk! She tried to talk him out of this gamble. Bill wouldn't listen to her. The business he purchased functioned well for about one year. Then things started to deteriorate. After two and a half years, Bill faced the fact that he would have to file bankruptcy. Karen knew nothing about this. Finally, the business closed.

One day, the youngest of their four children walked into the dark garage and could hardly breathe because of the exhaust fumes. She found her father sitting unconscious in his running car. Paramedics were called to the scene. Bill was saved from death. Karen visited him in the hospital the next day. She said to him, "Bill, you're a real failure! You've failed in everything you've ever tried in life. You even failed to kill yourself. I think you should know I've been to an attorney this morning, and am filing for divorce. I can't take this kind of life with you anymore."

Yes, money can cause people to do some pretty drastic things! This couple eventually divorced. Like Don and Ruth, they tried counseling. Again, things had apparently gone too far downhill. By the time they went to a counselor, they had already decided on divorce.

These are only three areas which are considered leading factors in deteriorating relationships. There are many others: children growing up and leaving the "nest," health problems, external familial problems, simply growing apart, religious or cultural differences, differences in parenting, career opportunities, mid-life crises, and so forth.

However, common to *all* of these areas is a breakdown in communication. Once communication is restored, the relationship can go through a definite healing process.

However, as has been mentioned, too often these problems just "slide" until one partner, or both, wants a divorce. For most situations counseling is a definite plus. But once people reach the point of no return, little else can be done.

But perhaps there is something that can help. Dr. William Hulme believes there should be a certain "cooling off" period. He wrote, "Helping people see that they are in no condition to make drastic decisions when they are emotionally upset may provide the necessary postponement that initiates the conditions that may lead to reconciliation." (*The Pastoral Care of Families,* Abingdon Press, 1962). This brief period of time may prove to be therapeutic to the family even though it doesn't lead directly to reconciliation.

When counseling can and should be seen as a therapeutic means of restoring a relationship, it cannot and should not be seen as a final step before divorce. It is possible for counseling to fail, but with a cooling off period, there is something that can still be done for the entire family as they go through the painful process of divorce and separation. That process is mediation.

CHAPTER THREE
Limitations of Court-ordered Mediation

JANET AND DAVID

The notice of court-ordered mediation came as a relief to Janet.

She wanted her children back.

Janet felt she had made mistakes. She had given David the custody of Dee and David, Jr. just to complete the divorce. She reflected on those stressed-out months before the divorce.

Her new dress shop on Wilshire Boulevard in Los Angeles was finally showing a profit, but she was spending days, evenings, and weekends there to manage it—unless she was with Michael. Michael was helping her believe in herself again. She had needed a break from the children to start her own business and rebuild her life.

But now things had changed. The divorce had come, and social workers were involved. There were interviews, lies, and gossip. Mediation was a last hope. Janet doubted it would work, but it was worth an effort. She wanted one thing out of the mediation—the kids back.

The date of the first mediation was three weeks away. The name of the mediator looked unfamiliar. As Janet's eyes glanced across the notice, she read the instructions for the first meeting. She hoped David had received the same information. He would have to bring the children's school and medical records—she didn't have them. The notice also stated that David and she weren't to talk outside the mediator's office, unless it was to exchange the children.

Janet wondered what mediation was all about. She wondered if Michael should come. She hoped so. She called her attorney to let her know that the court had ordered mediation. Her attorney explained that she would not be in touch with her during the mediation process unless the need arose, but would be available to review any final papers.

Janet brought Michael to the first session. David sat across from her in the waiting room. He was alone. She looked at the plaques on the wall. "J. William Barnett," the plaque read. Admitted to the California Bar, April 15, 1972.

Janet was intimidated when a tall, slightly graying man appeared and asked if he could speak to Janet and David.

"May Michael join me?" Janet asked.

"I'm sorry," Mr. Barnett stated, "only the parents of the children will be involved in mediation."

Janet asked Michael to wait for her. She anticipated the session would take about an hour.

Janet and David sat around a large, circular table. The mediator grabbed his file and sat down. After introducing himself, he told Janet and David to make themselves comfortable and offered them a cup of coffee.

"I hope we can work well together," he said. "I realize that the two of you have differences, but what we want to accomplish here is to find out what you can agree upon. I'm looking at my calendar, and I would like to establish a schedule for mediation over the next six weeks."

"Can't we get this whole matter concluded today?" Janet asked in response.

"The first step in mediation is to establish a schedule. If we can get everything concluded before the six weeks is up, that would be fine. The rest of the appointments will then be cancelled, but for right now I would like the two of you to agree on a time, place, date, and commitment to attend six sessions. Is that possible?"

"I'm working days. Can't really take time from work," David said.

"Can you arrange to work later in the day to make up for those hours?" the mediator inquired.

"I'll have to talk to my boss," David said.

"There is a court order to mediate," the mediator reminded him. "That means you will find the time. I want to be flexible with you. If you were to get the hours, what hours would your boss be most likely to give you?"

"Early in the morning seems to be best." The parties agreed to 9:00 on Mondays.

"You're doing fine," Mr. Barnett said. "You've agreed to six sessions of mediation and that's exciting not only for you, but for your children."

Janet and David agreed to share the cost of the mediator. Each would pay for their own lawyer. Janet and David also agreed upon a plan for Janet to see the kids the following weekend.

"I haven't seen the kids in two months," Janet said, "It'll be great to be with them."

The mediator gave David and Janet some instructions, and explained his role as mediator. "I'm not here as a counselor or an arbitrator. Mediation is to help the two of you decide." Mr. Barnett explained that all sessions would be confidential, and that he would in no manner represent either of them individually. David and Janet signed an agreement that the mediator would not be called into court to testify.

"I'm asking you to only communicate with me during mediation sessions when both of you are present," Mr. Barnett instructed.

Janet and David cordially said good-bye as they left the office. Michael was waiting for Janet. He stood and asked her how the session had gone.

"We're not to discuss mediation sessions, Michael," Janet said. "The mediator asked us not to. I hope you will understand that David and I need to work this one through."

Janet knew he was feeling left out. It was an uncomfortable feeling, but she needed to give mediation her all. Nothing had worked before. Maybe the hostility, name-calling, and gossip would be less—this time around.

David drove the children to Janet's home for the weekend. Accustomed to her nasty comments about their dad, the children asked if she was all right.

Janet explained, "You know I want you kids to come and live with me. Your father and I are going through mediation to attempt to work out what is right. I don't know what will happen, but we don't want to continue the fighting. It's too hard on you—and on us. Now let's just have some fun this weekend. OK?" The kids agreed.

David apologized for arriving late to the next mediation session. Janet was steaming. The mediator skillfully worked out the time and date difficulties. David agreed to be on time the next week. Janet wasn't so sure. David was late to everything.

The second session included an exchange of information about the children. David spoke about Dee. He described her as an enjoyable, active five-year-old with no major adjustment problems, but he felt Janet needed to spend more time with her daughter.

"She misses you, Janet," David said.

Janet felt guilty. She could only hope that her frequent absences would leave no permanent scars in her little girl's life. Someday she would explain.

"Somedays are now," Mr. Barnett explained to Janet. "Regardless of where Dee will live, both of you need to be involved in your children's lives. The two of you can best decide where she will live."

"I thought there was a preference for the mother?" Janet asked.

"That's old law," Mr. Barnett said. "Besides, in mediation we're not so concerned about the law. We're more concerned about what you believe is fair."

Then Mr. Barnett posed a question to David, "If your daughter were to come home from kindergarten with some exciting news, what would you say if she asked, 'Can I call my mother and tell her?'"

"I'd let her know that she could tell her mother on the weekend."

Janet gave a similar response.

"What effect would that have on the child?" Mr. Barnett asked.

"She'd probably be disappointed, but kids get disappointed for only a short time and then it goes away," Janet said.

"Would it hurt if she called right then?"

"Probably not," David concluded, and Janet nodded.

Mr. Barnett asked Janet and David to think about their relationship with Davie, Jr. for the next session. Both knew that session would be more difficult. David, Jr., 13, was a good looking young man, but there were problems: his grades were poor and he was hanging out with a rough crowd. They feared he was experimenting with drugs, and that they were losing control.

"Last week we talked about Dee," Mr. Barnett began. "This week we'll talk about David, Jr. How is your relationship with your son, David?"

"It's all right. Nothing spectacular, but at least I've been there for him, when Janet was all wrapped up in her boyfriend. I know David doesn't like Nancy, my new live-in girlfriend, but he can't tell me how to run my life."

Then Mr. Barnett asked Janet about her relationship with Davie, Jr.

"I love him," she said, getting teary-eyed, "but I've seen so little of him the past three years, it's almost as though I don't have a son anymore. I stopped calling him on the phone when we no longer had anything to talk about. Davie's always been quiet, and I just couldn't figure out what was happening. I guess there was too much going on in my life to know what was going on with Davie. One thing I know. Michael spends time with Davie. That's more than David does. That's why I believe we could give Davie a new chance."

David slammed his fist down. "This is the kind of gratitude I get. I'm the one who was there when you took off and left the kids with me. You said you needed a new change—one you were denied when you got pregnant and we had to marry. You said you didn't want the kids. Thanks a lot for telling me I messed up Davie's life and you're going to be the one to step in and get it straight."

David got up to leave. Mr. Barnett beat him to the door. "Before you leave, remember you committed yourself to six sessions, and I intend to hold you to them. You're not sitting here because of Janet. You're here because of your children."

David sat down. He was noticeably silent the rest of the time. Janet feared at the close of the third session that mediation was over. Like the social service visits, like all the court hearings, something always triggered anger and hatred. She left Mr. Barnett's office disillusioned. What was she to do? Couldn't David admit he just couldn't handle Davie anymore? Why couldn't he just swallow his pride?

Yes, David had been there when she had left the family. That was over three years ago. Yes, it was David who tried to keep a home for those kids. She vowed she would thank him for those years at the next session.

David did not come to the next session. Janet waited for an hour until Mr. Barnett dismissed her. He couldn't be located at home or work. Mr. Barnett sent out a letter circling the date of the next conference. Mr. Barnett also stated in the letter that a failure to mediate could have an adverse effect on the judge's decision regarding custody.

The next week David appeared. He looked worn. He looked much older than his 42 years.

This time Janet was the one to begin. "David, I've never told you how much I appreciate what you've done for Dee and Davie. When I couldn't make head nor tails out of my own life, you took those kids. I was 30, in love with Michael, and thought I had the answers to everything. You really were great for them. You've shown them a lot of love."

David broke down. "Davie's been arrested for theft of an automobile and possession of marijuana. There will be a court appearance tomorrow."

The room was silent. Janet didn't realize how much trouble David was in. She knew he had trouble with his grades in school, but she couldn't imagine that he was now involved in criminal activities.

The mediator asked both of them to attend the court hearing. The session was adjourned until the following week at which time Janet and David announced to the mediator that Davie would be living with Janet for awhile. Probation officers would check on him weekly, and all three of them would be involved in family therapy.

Janet and David decided Dee should remain with her father for the rest of the school year, and during the summer she would be with her mother.

Mr. Barnett asked Janet and David to return the following week to review an agreement that he would draft reflecting their desires. The following week, Janet and David orally agreed to the mediated agreement on the children.

During the next year, Janet and David worked through the struggles of their children. Dee eventually came to live with her mother. Janet broke up with Michael, realizing that he didn't like the kids as much as he had let on, and she took on a partner in her clothing store so she could spend more time with her children.

David adopted a faithful schedule of seeing his children, arranged through mediation. He became more sensitive to the children's needs.

Janet has regrets. Regrets about her divorce, the fighting between David and herself. Regrets about the children and the years she wasn't there for them. She arranged for an appointment with her pastor just to talk things over. She discovered he knew little about her or their family struggles even though she had been a member there for years.

She began, "I'm divorced, you know. I'm sorry for the mistakes I've made. I'm sorry for what this divorce has done to my children."

"I'm sure you are," the pastor responded. "But don't feel bad about it. It seems that everyone is divorced these days." His comments were pleasant, but Janet felt unheard.

The pastor was interrupted twice about an event scheduled for that evening. Janet decided she didn't want to take any more of his time and excused herself. Outside the walls of the imposing church building, Janet felt as hollow as the insides of a decayed tree. Surely there was a word of forgiveness that she could receive from God, from the church. But where could she find it? She needed to say good-bye to her past so that she could go on with her life.

THE BENEFITS OF MEDIATION

What are the benefits of mediation that have given lawmakers and divorcing couples new hope? Here are some of them.

Fairness

What is fair? Ask two people and you will get two different responses. Ask different judges and you will get different responses. Lawmakers establish what the majority believes fair by enacting legislation, but the constant change in laws is a clear indication of how nebulous and changeable the idea of "fair" really is.

Mediation allows a couple to decide for themselves what is fair. The couple does not have to accept what a judge might determine is fair, but may instead rely on their own resources and wisdom to carve out a fair agreement.

The mediator is uniquely positioned to help the couple find workable and fair solutions.

What is fair when a couple is first divorced may not continue to be fair. Mediation sets a friendly forum in which to work through future changes that may be needed between a couple, even after the divorce is final. Because the couple knows how to work with mediation, it becomes an ideal choice to solve future problems, too.

Honesty

Unlike adversarial divorce which can require costly, time-consuming information gathering, mediation encourages an open, free exchange of critical information concerning property and children. Because the mediator cannot be called to testify in court, and because the mediator is not representing either husband or wife, an honest exchange of critical information is fostered and encouraged. This procedure saves time and reduces the need for costly discovery techniques that are used in adversarial divorce to obtain information.

Positive time management

Mediation is not quick, nor is it simple. Mediated divorce may take time, but unlike the negative waiting time involved in adversarial divorce, mediated divorce involves positive time management. A couple works settlement at their own pace—a pace dictated by neither court schedules nor lawyer delays.

Mediation may involve four to twelve sessions (more if necessary), but each session is specifically designed to help the couple positively and creatively place the pieces of the settlement puzzle together. It does not encourage a "let's get this miserable thing over with" mentality. Mediated divorce is positive time management. It is neither fight nor flight.

Reduces lawyer costs

One of the major reasons couples seek out mediation is to cut costs. In mediation, less money is spent on lawyers and complex legal procedures that may give only negative results anyway. Money spent on mediation is instead channeled toward a hope that an agreement can be reached in a peaceful, humane way.

Educates a couple in settlement techniques

When a couple decides to mediate marital differences, they make a commitment to attempt to work out their own questions, rather than relying on judges and lawyers to call the shots. They make a commitment to educate themselves in settlement techniques that the adversarial setting often cannot effectively teach or effectively accommodate. The couple can also be reassured that a safe place and setting exist through which future issues can be resolved. A couple educated in settlement strategy has lifelong tools for working out their problems.

Reduces future litigation

Until the economic commitments of a divorce settlement are completed, future court hearings are always a probability. The divorce hearing is rarely the end. In many instances, it is only the beginning of years of responsibility. Communication is critical, not only at the time of the divorce, but also in the future. Mediation can create a positive setting in which new plans can be made to replace unworkable old ones.

Subsequent marriages may alter a couple's view of the appropriateness of an earlier decision. The birth of other children may cloud issues and force a couple to review what was decided before. If a couple has worked effectively with mediation, they are more likely to seek out a mediator again when problems arise. Mediation can significantly reduce future litigation and give the couple a workable framework in which to resolve problems.

Effect on children

Children of divorce live with less anxiety when their parents actively work out solutions to problems. Mediation takes some of the stress out of divorce for children. Children, in mediation, aren't expected to pick their favorite parent and don't need to live in fear that they will be called to testify against their mom or dad.

Mediation has been shown to foster successful exchange of the children and regular support payments, both of which have positive effects on the children of divorce. A study by Donald Stall of the Northwest Mediation Service in Bellevue, Washington, concluded that children of parents who chose mediation showed little behavioral change. Those in nonmediated groups more often exhibited negative behavior (alcohol and drug abuse, running away) that had not existed before the separation.

Mediation is designed to help parents talk constructively about and to their children and to help them work out a plan that includes both parents in the future parenting role. Mediation takes the win-lose mindset out of adversarial child custody disputes. When children know their parents are using peaceful means of resolving problems, they can live in the assurance that both parents love them and want to be involved in their lives. Those positive results outweigh any contested custody court battle.

Mediation has met with such enthusiastic approval by lawmakers that child custody mediation has been made mandatory in many states.

Self-worth

Kids aren't the only ones reaping the benefits of mediated divorce, since the divorcing couple involved in mediation often also experiences an increase in their feelings of self-worth. When a couple decides for themselves what is best, they are more likely to feel positively about the outcome.

Mediation emphasizes the means by which settlement is reached as much as the end result. Adversarial divorce concentrates on the end results.

When mediation may not work

The positives of mediated divorce far outweigh the negatives, but it is important to realize that mediation may not be effective in all cases. When significant imbalances of power or physical abuse exist between the couple, or when emotions are too charged, counseling should first be utilized. It is always possible that after successful counseling, mediation may be appropriate. Some skilled mediators also believe mediation can be effective when abuse exists.

Secular mediation

Family mediation is an emerging profession and is rapidly gaining approval and support from both legal and behavioral science professionals. As recently as 1981, the Academy of Family Mediators of Eugene, Oregon was formed. Its major role was to set minimum standards of practice and training for professional mediators. The address is given in the Appendix.

Mediation has come of age, but how does that involve the church? Why should the church get involved? Isn't divorce something to be left to the courts and secular mediators? What does the church have that the courts of law and secular mediators can't accomplish? Part two gives some answers.

PART TWO
A Biblically-based Alternative

CHAPTER FOUR
Mediation in the Church

Randy and Sue

Randy sat in Pastor Dan's office waiting for a miracle to happen. His entire world was falling apart. He knew he had himself to blame, but couldn't understand his own reasons for wanting to jeopardize his marriage to Sue. He looked at his pastor and said, "Dan, I don't know why I did the things I did, but I have to get Sue back. You have to help me. You're the last chance I have." Pastor Dan looked confused as Randy recalled the events that led to his desperation.

♦ ♦ ♦

"Sue," Randy called up from the basement. "I can't find my golf shoes. I thought I left them in the laundry room."

"They're in the closet when they belong, Randy—up here!" laughed Sue.

Randy was always leaving things somewhere—just like the kids. In addition to their nine-year-old son and sixteen-year-old daughter, Sue said that she also had a forty-year-old child.

Randy and Sue were a couple who worked hard during their 18-year marriage. They weren't a struggling couple. But they worked hard to get where they were. They lived in a small town in Illinois about 20 miles south of Chicago. They had just completed their "dream home" which they both designed. And with the exception of the actual construction of the frame of the house, the electrical work, and the plumbing, they did all the work themselves. The house became a showpiece for the entire town. Randy and Sue were proud and pleased with their accomplishment.

Their two children shared in every delight of their parents. Sarah, the 16-year-old, was exceptionally close to her dad. Some people would have called her a "tomboy." Ever since she was little, she accompanied her dad on fishing trips and would occasionally be his "caddy" when he went golfing. Sarah was a beautiful young lady who was now starting to date. She did well in school and was considered a leader in her junior class. But surprisingly, her priority was still to spend as much time with her dad as possible. She enjoyed the outdoors, and she had a respect for her dad that most fathers just dream of. Randy knew the day would come when her priorities would change, and he knew that day was coming soon.

Kevin was their mischievous nine-year-old son. Sue often said, "If Kevin had been our first child, I think we would have thought twice about having a second! He keeps us jumping all the time." Truer words were never spoken. From the time he was born, Kevin insisted on as much attention as parents would normally give to five children. He would come home with frogs in his pocket, friends for dinner, and notes from the teacher (not always good). He brought laughter into the house. Kevin was not by any standards a naughty or bad child, just *active*. Since Sue was the one who was at home, Kevin developed a genuine closeness to his mom.

However, both children were close to both of their parents. They were a happy home, filled with the hustle and bustle typical of the average middle class family.

Randy was senior accountant at a prominent accounting firm in Chicago. Even though it was a long trip to work every day, Randy and Sue both felt this was the price to pay for having their children grow up in a small town. Because Randy was so tied to his family, it was a rare occurrence for him to be home any later than 6:00 in the evening. While others in his office would ask him to go for a drink after work, Randy would always turn them down in preference to being home with his family. Randy also was a well-rounded outdoorsman. He was particularly fond of fishing and would always be the one to make the suggestion to the family to take off for a few days and go to his parent's lake cabin and relax with some fishing. Five years ago, Randy also developed a new interest: golf. Because of his natural athletic ability, he caught on to the game with ease. He was one of the top contenders in various golf tournaments in the area.

Sue was the "dedicated" homemaker. No one could ever challenge her for being the kind who would sit around all day drinking coffee and watching soap operas. Sue worked hard around their new home and cleaned meticulously. When she wasn't working on the house, she would be running with the kids, especially Kevin. She also made time for her bridge club which met every two weeks, shared Randy's interest in golf, and was in the women's club. While her abilities were not on the same scale as Randy's, she enjoyed getting out of the house and breaking up her routine.

Life for this family was uncomplicated and uncluttered. They were active in their local church. Both Randy and Sue grew up in different religious backgrounds: Sue a Lutheran, and Randy a Presbyterian. They had "compromised" and joined the Episcopal church. Randy eventually became a deacon and Sue took part in the "social concerns" committee. Both took their church membership very seriously, and made sure that they hardly missed a Sunday. Sarah and Kevin were involved in the Christian education program of the church. The only time church attendance was ever in question was during one of Randy's fishing trips.

On a Friday afternoon in late June, Randy came home from work and announced that he was going fishing. First, he eagerly told Sarah, since she often accompanied him on his weekend trips.

"Gee, Dad," she said. "I've got a date this weekend with Rick. Maybe some other time."

"What?" Randy thought. "Sarah's turning me down? I can't really *make* her go."

As usual, Sue and Kevin didn't really feel like going. Besides, Kevin had planned to go bowling with one of his friends.

Sue said, "Why don't you go without us. You deserve some time alone, anyway. You might even enjoy it."

"Well, it's something I haven't done for a long time. Work has been kind of stressful lately. If it's all right with you, Sue, I will go. I'll leave tonight and be home by Sunday night."

While getting ready to go, Randy passed a mirror in their bedroom. He looked at his graying temples, some new wrinkles he hadn't noticed, and a face that was starting to show some wear and tear. He remembered the days when Sarah would just jump at the chance to go fishing with him, while Sue and Kevin would drop everything just so they could be together as a family.

Obsessed with the thought of getting old, Randy loaded the car for a relaxing weekend alone. But he was depressed at the thought of being alone. He felt deserted. On his way to the cabin, he remembered he left at his office some new tackle he purchased recently. He figured he would stop there, pick up the tackle, and try it out this weekend.

He arrived at his office building and took the elevator to the floor he worked on. He noticed there were lights on in the office complex.

"Who could be working this late?" he thought.

He walked into his office and noticed Rita, one of the secretaries, at her desk. She was working late so she could get all the correspondence out of the way and have a nice, relaxing weekend, free of any worry.

"Hi, Rita, I'm surprised you're working so late. I didn't think anyone would be here this late," said Randy.

"Oh," Rita said. "I just had some loose ends to take care of around here. And I didn't want the thought of leaving them undone haunting me the entire weekend."

"Boy, that's what I call real dedication," said Randy. "I suppose a nice looking girl like you has lots of plans for weekends."

"Actually, the men I prefer to date are a little older than I. And the market is pretty slim for me, since most older men are happily married."

Randy started thinking to himself that it was ridiculous for a young woman in her 20s to have such a boring weekend to look forward to. He became envious of her youth, and even envious of her freedom.

Here she sits complaining to me that she is bored with her social life, he thought. *She should be in my shoes. Just wait 'til she turns 40. She'll wish she had dated men her age. I know one thing, I would be the first in line if I were closer to her age—and single, of course.*

"What are you doing here?" Rita asked.

"Well, I'm headed up to the cabin to do some fishing, and on my way I remembered I left some new tackle in my desk," he said. "I just love fishing," she replied. "My dad took me fishing a lot when I was growing up."

"Well, I just gave my daughter the same opportunity, and she turned me down."

"I can't imagine that! If I had a father who would want me to go with him for the weekend, I would jump at the chance. Besides, does she realize how proud she should be to be seen with such a good looking man as you?"

Hmmmm, Randy thought. *Is she making a pass at me, an about-to-become-old man?*

"I guess she has better things to do now," Randy said with composure.

"Well, what better thing is there to do than to be with you?"

"Rita, I can't believe you're saying this."

"Well, you're just the type of man I've been looking for my entire life. It's too bad you're married," Rita added.

"Well," Randy said, "I'm flattered you would even look at an old man like me."

"Are you kidding?" Rita laughed. "I've been trying to get you to notice me for months!"

"Even though you know I am married?" Randy asked.

"Why should that stop anyone from wishing?" Rita said.

"Well, you mentioned you liked fishing, and I'm not crazy about going alone. Why don't you come with me?"

And that's how it all began. Rita went with Randy that weekend. And any opportunity Randy could manage, he spent time with Rita.

About three months after their first trip to the cabin, Randy and Rita decided they would spend a weekend together again. This time they had to be more careful so Sue's suspicions wouldn't be aroused. Randy told Sue that he and his friend, Tim, were going fishing on Friday and would be gone until Sunday.

"Randy, would you like us to go with you?" asked Sue.

Randy was shocked that, for a change, they wanted to go fishing with him, so he had to think fast.

"Sue, Tim would really feel out of place if I took my family and there he would be without anyone."

"Well," Sue said, "I just don't want you thinking that we're losing interest in going with you. But I understand that you and Tim would probably get a lot more fishing done without us tagging along."

Randy breathed a sigh of relief. He told Sue not to worry about a thing and said they would be back Sunday evening.

Sure enough, Randy was true to his word. He came back on Sunday evening. He was in a good mood as well.

"Did you have a nice weekend?" Sue asked.

"It was great. Tim and I didn't catch too many fish, but we had a good time just talking and joking around."

"I didn't think you would catch many fish. You left all your fishing gear at home," Sue said, glaring at Randy.

Randy's heart went up in his throat. He was speechless! What kind of excuse should he make up? How much did Sue know? Had she checked his story out with Tim?

Finally Randy mustered up enough courage and said, "Sue, it's not what it looks like. I just had to get away on my own. I need more freedom. I need to find myself before I get too old."

It wasn't long after that conversation that Randy decided to make an appointment with his pastor. He was confused. He didn't know what to do or where to turn.

Randy went to his pastor's office the afternoon of the appointment ready to pour his heart out. He walked into the pastor's study, sat down, and stared at the floor. After Randy had sat down, Pastor Dan walked into his office and was surprised to see that the normally neat Randy was replaced by a tired looking, sloppily dressed person who gave the appearance of not having had a decent meal in days, a change of clothes, or adequate sleep. There was a long silence. Finally Randy blurted out, "I want a divorce, and I don't know how I'm going to ask Sue. Will you help me?"

Pastor Dan was stunned. He thought, *Is this for real? What should I say? What can I do? How can I fix this?*

"Why?" he finally asked.

"I don't know," Randy replied.

Pastor Dan thought, *That's great, I've got a guy in here who thinks he knows what he wants, but doesn't know why. I wonder if he has both oars in the water. I wonder what else is going on.*

Breaking the silence, Pastor Dan said, "If you don't know the reasons, I don't understand how you came to the conclusion of divorce."

"I just don't love her anymore."

"I don't understand. How can you draw that conclusion? You and Sue always seem so happy, so content. Have you been fighting a lot lately?"

"No," Randy replied. "We get along just fine. By the way, you better know—I'm seeing another woman."

"Does Sue know?"

"No, I don't think so. Pastor, do you think you could tell her? She would react better if it came from you."

Pastor Dan was shocked. *This guy can't be serious. What does he expect out of me?* He said, "Why don't you and Sue both come in and we can talk this whole problem out?"

The next day Sue came to the pastor's study with Randy. Although she thought a lot about the "mysterious" weekend, she tried to push it into the recesses of her mind. Sue did not like to deal with problems. She wanted her family to be seen as the "perfect" family. If there were any problems, Randy could deal with them. She appeared totally unsuspecting as she walked into Pastor Dan's office with Randy. They both sat down.

"Randy told me you wanted to talk to us," Sue began. "If it's about helping out more in the church, our schedules are so busy that—"

"No," Pastor Dan interrupted. "I think Randy has some pretty serious things for the three of us to talk about."

Randy didn't respond. Dan looked at Randy and thought, *You're not going to get by this easily.* Pastor Dan's direct stare at Randy prompted Randy to speak.

"I want a divorce."

"What did you say?" Sue asked.

"I want a divorce," Randy stated again, still staring at the floor.

"Wait a minute. Back up," Sue said. "You brought me in here to tell me you want a divorce? You've got to be kidding! No, I can see you're not kidding. Why?"

"I don't know," Randy replied.

"I know you better than that," Sue replied. "Should I tell you something?"

"OK."

"I think you're seeing another woman. I've known that for a long time." This time it was Randy who was shocked.

"Give me credit for having some brains," Sue said. "When you come home consistently late from work. When you decide to make these little trips Saturday and Sunday afternoons to the store. When you totally give up interests in hobbies and church. When you totally ignore Sarah and Kevin. And finally when you told this big lie about going fishing with Tim. Don't you think I checked out your story? Do you think I'm a moron?"

Pastor Dan met with the couple several times. Randy finally left home. Sue was extremely bitter and angry. She sought a restraining order from the court forbidding Randy from entering the home. Sue continued to receive counseling. She was just beginning to make some progress in her life when things started to change again. She decided to go through with the divorce. *After all,* she kept thinking, *this is what Randy wants.* So the divorce hearing was scheduled.

During this time, Randy decided he would pay Pastor Dan a visit at the parsonage. For the first time in months, Randy showed some emotion. He broke down in tears.

"Pastor, I don't want a divorce. I don't know what came over me. I have left Rita. I've got to have Sue back."

"Great," Pastor Dan said. "Let's give Sue a call and see if she can meet us here right now."

Sue agreed to meet them at the church office. Randy began this session as soon as Sue was seated.

"Sue, I'm so sorry for what I've put you through. I love you so much. Please, please take me back."

There was rage in Sue's eyes. "Are you kidding?" she screamed. "After everything you've put me through?" Sue stood up, turned around, and stormed out of Pastor Dan's office. Randy was speechless.

Pastor Dan was speechless too, but he wondered, *Where do we go from here? Isn't there anywhere to turn?*

What tools does the church have to offer in a case like this? What should we be doing as the body of Christ? Can there be a reconciliation? Is there any hope? Can two people treat one another with enough respect so that problems can be talked out? Is divorce the only answer?

Mediation

Sue and Randy secured their own attorneys. In frustration, Pastor Dan went to his bishop, Dr. Benson.

"Dr. Benson, I'm at the point of total frustration. Two very close friends of mine are seeking a divorce. The wife is totally dead set against any possibility of reconciliation. The husband wants to get back together. And I don't want to take sides. I know that if they could receive the right kind of guidance, they can at least settle things in a halfway decent manner."

"Dan, divorce is one of the most frustrating issues to deal with in the ministry. I think I might have an idea as to how to make their lives a little more bearable through this painful ordeal. It could also be a good tool for you to use in the future."

"Well, I'm all ears," Dan said.

"Dan, have you ever heard of divorce mediation?"

"Sure, that's when a neutral party mediates differences between the husband and wife. But I'm not so sure that they are at this point in their dispute."

"What point are they at?" Bishop Benson asked.

"Sue wants to get even with Randy for being unfaithful to her, and Randy is going through a lot of guilt and remorse over his infidelity."

"Do you see that there could be a possibility of a reconciliation?"

"Well," Dan said, "I'm not too sure that they will ever get back together again, but I see a possibility of the two of them working things out in a more peaceful way. And I know that the attorneys are out to represent their clients with very little effort to reconcile their differences."

"Dan, I would like to make a suggestion. How would you feel if the church could be more involved in the mediation?"

"I know that the church has mixed feelings about divorce. And I know we have very few resources to draw on in terms of divorce. There is always the possibility of intense counseling. But in Randy and Sue's complicated case, counseling is not an alternative at this point because Sue will not go along with it."

"But Dan, don't you think the church could be a valuable instrument for mediation in troubled relationships?" Bishop Benson asked.

"I guess I never thought of that. We automatically think of mediation as being a part of our legal system. But it would make sense since we are so often the ones who marry the couples. Maybe we should take more responsibility in the lives of the couples even if that means divorce."

"I would suggest a person who deals with Christian divorce mediation. His name is Mark Scheller. Mark's occupation is in the area of Christian counseling. However, he has become involved and is now certified in the new area of Christian divorce mediation. I think you should go and speak with Mark. I know he can give you some good, sound advice in dealing with this troubled couple. It is possible that you have become too emotionally involved in this particular case. Maybe the help from an 'outsider' is just what this couple needs."

Pastor Dan called Mark as soon as he returned to his office. Mark was interested in meeting Randy and Sue.

"Do you think you could get this couple to come into my office as soon as possible?" Mark asked.

"I don't know," Dan said. "All I can do is try."

Mediation in the Church

"Remind them that mediation can help them to agree on basic and fundamental things in their relationship without going through all the legal hassles. It is also a biblical way of solving disputes. Remind them that they are two adults who care about their children. It is their responsibility to one another and to their children to try to come to the most peaceful and workable solution for them."

Dan had a lot to think about. To say the least, he was very apprehensive about approaching Randy and especially Sue with this proposition. But his choices were limited! And after all, he wasn't bringing them to a counselor who was going to try to preserve their marriage. He was bringing them to a third party who would be objective.

Dan thought he would first try Sue. After all, it was Sue who wanted the divorce so badly. If she didn't agree, then there was no point in trying Randy.

"Sue," Pastor Dan said on the telephone, "I wonder if I could—"

"If it's to talk about my marriage and counseling, the answer is a firm no." Sue said emphatically.

"No, I know you're against any type of counseling. But there is an alternative that I wasn't even aware of until today," Dan said.

"Dan, the only alternative for me is a divorce. Did you hear me? I'm so sick and tired of everyone trying to bring me and *that man* back together!"

"Sue, there are some things that you and Randy *have* to talk about. I'm willing to set up an appointment for you and Randy to talk to a third party."

"You aren't listening to me," Sue said. "I have nothing to talk to Randy about. We have attorneys to take care of those things."

"Sue," Dan said, "wouldn't it be great if you could settle these things *before* taking them into court? You have two children who are really broken up over this whole matter. They feel so torn. They feel they have no voice in what happens to their family. Don't you owe this, at least, to your children and to your 20-year relationship? I know that children are the wrong reason for staying together. But don't you think your whole family deserves to be treated fairly? The person I have in mind to refer you to is trained in the area of mediation. He is not there to 'patch things up' for you. He is there to help you arrive at peaceful means of settling various issues for you and Randy. He will not preach to or lecture either one of you. He will simply listen and mediate. This is one responsibility that the church can take part in. Why don't you give it a try?"

Sue hesitated for a long time but finally said, "I guess I do owe this much to my children. But I'm not going to get back together with Randy. I mean that, too!"

Pastor Dan, while sensing a lot of bitterness, was basically pleased with Sue's response. And, as expected, he had no trouble convincing Randy that this was the thing to do. Dan cautioned Randy, "Don't get your hopes up. We are not using this as a means of getting you and Sue back together. We are simply trying to settle things in a peaceful way. This should be the Christian response."

Dan gave Mark Scheller's phone number to Sue. It was Sue who set up the appointment. She did all of her communication with Randy, though, through Pastor Dan. Dan told Randy the location of Mark's office, and the time Sue had scheduled. Even though he had to take time off from his job, Randy was agreeable. Sue and Randy met in the waiting room at Mark's office.

"Hi, Sue," Randy said. "I've really missed you a lot. How've you been?" It had been several months since they had even talked.

Mediation in the Church 85

"I don't think we have anything to talk about. I came here to talk to a 'third party' about divorce. I didn't really come here to talk to the likes of you," Sue said.

"Sue, don't you think it's time for you to forgive and forget?"

"Randy, if we weren't in someone else's office, I would slap you across the face! How dare you talk to me about forgiveness! How dare you think—"

Just then, a man came into the waiting room. It was, of course, their mediator. "Hello, my name is Mark Scheller. Hopefully, we'll be able to pick up on the animated conversation you were just having. Let's continue it in my office."

Randy and Sue followed Mark into his office. Sue sat in a chair opposite Randy. She wanted to sit as far from him as possible!

Mark began the conversation, "I have learned a few of the details from your pastor. But let's start at the beginning. Why don't you tell me about your marriage. First of all, how long have you been married?"

"Nineteen, almost twenty years," Randy said.

"To think I wasted twenty years of my life living with him," Sue said, looking at Mark. She refused to even look at Randy.

"You have two children?"

"Yes," Sue said. "They are the only good things that came out of our sick relationship."

"Oh, come on, Sue," Randy said. "You can't just throw twenty years away thinking they were all that bad. We had some good years together. We were happy. Then I made one little mistake, and you have decided all of a sudden you want nothing more to do with me."

"Little mistake?" Sue screamed. "Do you mean to tell me that what you did was just a *little* mistake? Oh, come on, Randy, you can do a lot better than that. Even I give you more credit for having more brains than that!"

"All right, a big mistake. But before then, we had a pretty good relationship. We were a close family. We loved being together. We loved doing things together."

"But you took care of that, Randy. You avoided us like we had the plague. Kevin and Sarah even noticed that. That 'little' mistake is costing us our entire marriage."

"Where do Kevin and Sarah stand in all of this?" asked Mark. "I know they still love me," said Randy. "I see them every Saturday, and it breaks my heart to say 'good-bye' to them. They keep talking about Sue and me getting back together. I keep telling them that if it were up to me, we would be giving our marriage a try."

"Yes, thanks to you—and because you say things like that—our children resent me," Sue said.

"Do they resent you, or is it just that they don't understand the total scope of what happened in your relationship?" Mark asked.

"I told them all about Rita, the woman I *was* seeing," Randy said.

"And how did they respond?" Mark asked.

"At first, Sarah wouldn't even talk to me. Kevin didn't really understand what it was all about. Finally, they both forgave me. I would think that Sue could work on a little forgiveness, too."

"I could what?" Sue responded. "You mean to tell me that I could forgive you—Would you understand, Randy, if the shoe were on the other foot?"

"I can see we're not getting anywhere," Mark said. "I'm not here to make your marriage work again. I'm here to insure that issues can be worked out peacefully. You see, Sue, you have made the decision that divorce is your only option. I can understand your bitterness and anger. But it is our goal to remove some of that bitterness and anger so that we can go on with our lives. There is one thing for sure: that even though there is the probability of divorce, life still goes on for both of you. We are here to talk about forgiveness and a peaceful means of settling this dispute. Now for the sake of your future and the future of your own children whom both of you love, are you willing to try to settle this matter in a peaceful way? We have to remember that Christ is with us and wanting to work in and through us. But we have to let his Spirit work! We cannot rule out reconciliation even though you're talking about divorce. Forgiveness, even in a divorce, needs to be part of the picture. And forgiveness is biblical. Even though divorce is the primary issue, we cannot rule out all other options. Are both of you willing to forgive one another?"

"If I were willing to forgive," Sue said, "we wouldn't be here, would we?"

"That's right. But you still have a lot of issues to deal with," Mark said. "And the sooner we work on this goal of forgiveness, the quicker we can get down to the business of mediating your differences."

"I think you're asking the impossible of Sue, Mark," Randy said. "I deserve what Sue is feeling. I was so wrong, dead wrong in what I did. I can't even explain why I did it. The one thing I do know is that I love Sue more than anyone could ever imagine. I have prayed for forgiveness from God over and over again. And I know that he has forgiven me. But I am having trouble with forgiving myself. So I can certainly understand why Sue will not forgive me."

"Sue, can you forgive Randy?" Mark asked.

"It's not a matter of being able to forgive Randy. It's a matter of wanting to forgive him. It's a matter of pride. It's a matter of trusting him. It's even a matter of getting even with him," Sue said through her tears.

"Do you love Randy?" Mark asked.

"I don't think that's the issue at all. I would say that I loved Randy at one time. But I just want to get things settled now and get on with my life."

"All right, are both of you willing to work at settling the issues that are pressing now, like working together for the benefit of the children, division of property, visitation rights, child support, college educations for the children?" Mark said.

"It all seems so final and cold," said Sue. "But I guess these are the issues that we have to face."

"As much as I want to fight to keep my marriage," said Randy, "I suppose I should be realistic enough to realize that we have a lot of issues to settle."

Randy and Sue went to Mark's office for six appointments. By this time, they were on speaking terms. They seemed to have everything worked out in terms of financial support, visitation, and the involvement of their children. On the seventh visit, both Randy and Sue agreed that their children, Sarah and Kevin, should become involved in the process. The main reason for this was that they could witness the fact that their parents were settling differences in a peaceful and "adult" manner. Randy met Sue and the kids in the waiting room of Mark's office.

Sarah looked at her dad and said, "Dad, I've been praying so much for both you and mom. And now mom tells me that this hasn't been marriage counseling for you at all! I really had my hopes up. But now I realize that you were just working out your differences so that you could divorce in a peaceful way. I just don't understand why you and mom can't learn to love each other."

It was at this point that Mark appeared in the doorway of his office. "You must be Sarah, and you must be Kevin. I've heard a lot about the two of you. Come on in."

The foursome went into Mark's office. Mark didn't hesitate to say, "Sarah, I know that this is so hard to understand, but the one thing I do know is that both of your parents love you very much. And I know that you love your parents very much."

The family was with Mark for about one hour. They talked about the importance of forgiveness. They dealt with the various issues that were covered in the previous six sessions. Then out of the clear blue, Sue said, "I am realizing now what the word forgiveness really means. And Randy, it's taken some time, but—I do forgive you. I'm so confused. Where do we go from here? I don't even know if divorce is the answer anymore. Do you think we can try out our marriage again?"

Randy burst into tears. "Oh, Sue, I love you so much, and now you have given me hope. Yes, yes, I know we can work it out."

It was at that point that the entire family hugged each other, and cried. They cried "happy tears."

Then Mark said, "I hate to be the wet blanket, but you can't just jump into this relationship thinking that everything is all right, because it isn't. There are still feelings to be talked out, and a lot of issues to deal with."

"Wait a minute," said Randy, "I thought you were the one talking to us about forgiveness, and now you say we aren't ready to jump back into a relationship?"

"That's right," said Mark. "You need to go into counseling. I would suggest that you contact Pastor Dan and begin to work at rebuilding your marriage. The purpose for Christian divorce mediation is not to rebuild your marriage, only to seek out various issues to deal with and work at forgiveness. Mission accomplished! Now it's time for the two of you to put your lives back together."

Pastor Dan was overjoyed at the prospect of Randy and Sue staying together as a couple. But there were a lot of issues to be dealt with. There were many, many things in their marriage they were not even aware of that needed help. After four months of intense counseling with Pastor Dan, it was Randy who said, "Dan, we really appreciate all of the work you have done with us. Now it's time for us to see if we can work things out as a couple."

Dan told them, "Always remember that I am here. Let's not let things go so far that your marriage will be on the line again."

Sue then asked Pastor Dan, "Dan, we would like to have our vows renewed and would be so honored to have you officiate at this ceremony."

It was a real celebration. The family and close friends of Randy and Sue were invited to this wonderful ceremony. This time Randy and Sue listened very carefully to one another and to Pastor Dan when the vows were read. Sue and Randy both meant it when they promised to be faithful to one another in "good times and in bad."

It was Sarah who first congratulated her parents and said, "I feel that God has returned our parents to me and Kevin."

Pastor Dan said to her, "You have always had them, Sarah. But now he has given you parents who have a very special and different kind of love for one another that most couples only dream of."

There wasn't a dry eye in the congregation that day. A new meaning to marriage had been given to all who were present in the church.

IF THE MARRIAGE IS NOT SAVED

It should be kept in mind that Randy and Sue are probably not the "typical" example of Christian divorce mediation.

However, the process should always be open to the reconciliation of the couple and restoration of the marriage. But when that does not happen, it is possible for the couple to have an amicable divorce through this process. Because of Christ's grace and forgiveness which the church has to offer, Christian divorce mediation can provide the proper motivation for peaceful solutions. In 1 Corinthians 6, Paul wrote, "If any of you has a dispute with another, dare he take it before the ungodly for judgment instead of before the saints? ... The very fact that you have lawsuits among you means you have been completely defeated already" (vv. 1, 7).

The mediation process follows the admonition of Christ himself, "If your brother sins against you, go and show him his fault, just between the two of you. If he listens to you, you have won your brother over. But if he will not listen, take one or two others along, so that 'every matter may be established by the testimony of two or three witnesses.' If he refuses to listen to them, tell it to the church; and if he refuses to listen even to the church, treat him as you would a pagan or a tax collector" (Matt. 18:15-17). "Tell it to the church!" Divorce mediation is scriptural! Husband and wife do not have to settle differences in a secular court of law. Why would Jesus make such a statement? Because he saw the wonderful possibilities of reconciliation. In spite of the fact that some couples cannot see any possibility of remaining in a marriage relationship, they can once again see the amazing grace offered through the church as a means of amicably settling differences and proceeding with their futures and their lives.

Anyone who has gone through the pain of divorce will testify that usually there is not a clear "winner." Once again we are reminded of Paul's words, "The very fact that you have lawsuits among you means you have been completely defeated already." The hurt experienced when children are involved, for example, is indescribable. Children feel divided loyalties. They feel torn. They cry out for help. But who hears them? Many times, because of strong and strained feelings, their cries fall on deaf ears. Christian divorce mediation reminds parents of their obligations to their children throughout the entire process of divorce and separation. So often the bitterness toward the other parent is verbalized in front of the children (sometimes intentionally). Often, because children have such strong love, respect, and trust for their parents, they will listen to those harsh words and their feelings become bitter and confused. In *Five Cries of Parents,* Merton and Irene Strommen urged, "Parents should not blame each other; and they should stress that the children are not to blame for the divorce, that they are free to love both parents, and that they will not be asked to take sides against either parent" (Harper & Row, Publishers, 1985, p. 23). Because of the grace and forgiveness which the Christian church offers (and which this process offers), children can be happy, secure, and well-adjusted because of the wisdom both parents use in dealing with their children. Each of the parents can remind the children that they still have two parents, even though they may spend more time with one of them.

Christian divorce mediation could make an enormous impact on the lives of many families who are hurting, and the life of the Christian community in general. Four case studies have been provided for the reader. Three of these case studies did not involve Christian divorce mediation. Whatever the outcome, people who were hurting could have been helped by this process. The fourth case study of Randy and Sue had a "happy" ending. However, even if a divorce would have taken place, this couple could have used the tools given to them through the mediation process to arrive at peaceful decisions.

Christian divorce mediation places the emphasis on peacefully settling disputes among our community of faith. It is time for the church to see that it has so much to offer couples who are going through the anguish of conflict and hurt feelings. Our greatest and most wonderful asset is that we have Christ himself who wants so desperately to be a part of our lives "in good times and in bad."

CHAPTER FIVE
Mediation Is Biblical

"For this reason Christ is the mediator . . ." (Heb. 9:15). Mediation is offered through our secular legal system. In fact, there is evidence that this process is becoming more widely used and accepted. There are some things that could be added to the secular mediation process, but which are somewhat impossible to do because of the separation of church and state in our country. This is a golden opportunity for the church to step in, while the approach and concept is still relatively new and unique, with a fresh, grace-centered approach to divorce mediation. We can base this on the premise that in spite of differences which are probably beyond any help, we can still help people experiencing the pain of separation or divorce to find peaceful solutions. Hebrews 9 can be seen as a mandate for us to turn to Christ and ask him for help. Yes, he listens! He responds! He cares! He can help!

THE CHURCH AND RECONCILIATION

"I came that they may have life, and have it abundantly" (John 10:10). *Reconciliation* is one of the most beautiful and magnificent words in our English language. It is time for the church to stand up and be recognized as a means through which God can bring reconciliation to people. Reconciliation, the restoration of harmony, brings the peace by which people can work together toward agreeable and logical solutions.

Many of us know of people in our own communities, brothers and sisters, who have not spoken a word to each other since a parent's will was probated. We have known children who have run away from their parents in a fit of anger; their mothers and fathers wait in vain for some word of hope from their children.

Pastors and counselors will testify repeatedly that almost weekly they sit with a husband and wife who have lived together for years, whose lives and physical bodies have been joined in the most intimate type of relationship known to humankind. They have children whom they both love. And yet, between them, there is little or no communication. There is nothing but a horrible mistrust and possibly a hatred they both feel.

However, Christ towers over us, affirms our lives, and says in effect, "Come to me. Be reconciled to one another." If we can make available the systematic approach to church divorce mediation described in this book, we will see that it *can* bring couples to recognize their differences and move toward solving these differences.

Reconciliation is one of the most important tools we have to offer as the church of Jesus Christ. Secular society does not know of this type of mediation. In fact, the restoration of harmony is usually left up to counseling sessions which may or may not be mandated by secular mediation. Finding ways to work out solutions peaceably can help couples avoid some of the pain of divorce.

THE CHURCH AND DIVORCE

"His mother Mary was pledged to be married to Joseph . . ." (Matt. 1:18). Churches have the deserved reputation for being the responsible custodians of family statistics and records. In fact, many people will turn to church records when researching their family trees or when looking up a date as proof for legal documents. Marriages are a large part of the record keeping system we maintain in our church files. However, there is definitely a lack of any chronicled information dealing with divorces which have taken place. The church is here to let the Spirit of the living Jesus Christ work in and through members. And yet we have not let the work of Christ extend through each of us when it comes to the ugly business of divorce.

It is such a familiar sight in a congregation to see couples worshipping together with their children. However, when a couple goes through the pain of divorce, one or both of the spouses often cease to attend worship services. Why? One divorced woman complained, "They [the congregation] treat me like I have an advanced case of leprosy! So rather than make people feel uncomfortable—not to mention my own children—I am choosing not to attend church services for awhile. Maybe when things cool down a little, I'll return."

We have to see that the church of Jesus Christ has an amazing opportunity to minister to the needs of these families by becoming actively involved in the lives of its members. As Christ's servants, we cannot just close our eyes anymore. We cannot pretend that everything is going to be all right! No, our Lord is a realist. We have to fulfill our responsibility to every member, and let the Spirit of the living Jesus Christ work in and through all of us.

THE CHURCH AND PARENTS

"Fathers, do not embitter your children, or they will become discouraged" (Col. 3:21). While the only tool that separated couples have been able to utilize in the past has been the court system, we have seen that this system has not been able to solve the issues of child support and parental sharing. Proof of this comes from the lives of single mothers and fathers who are continually heard complaining about the lack of interest a former spouse shows to their children.

One woman who had been divorced for five years mentioned that while the father had provided financial support for their three children, he had not seen his children in more than two years. In another case, a man who had received custody of his son complained that though his ex-wife had not contacted their son for over five years, suddenly she was filing for custody!

Since most courts award "custody" to the mother, statistics are based on the support the father provides. These statistics reveal that approximately 60 percent of divorced fathers do not pay child support. In those cases, the entire financial stress of raising the children is left to one parent. Statistics also reveal that 49 percent of these same fathers have not seen their children in the past year. As is the case all too often, the children are the victims who suffer because of the lack of a third party to help mediate any of these differences.

The church cannot forget her children. We place an enormous responsibility on the congregation for the Christian growth of each child. For example, many baptismal services have a portion in which the congregation welcomes the child into the family of the church of Jesus Christ. Being a part of our family means that we accept the responsibility of caring for, loving, and nurturing the child.

THE CHURCH AND CHILDREN

"Children should not have to save up for their parents, but parents for their children" (2 Cor. 12:14). Yes, it is often the case that the forgotten ones in a marital dispute are the children. They are often the *real* victims of a painful divorce.

Divorce can be interpreted as a way of ridding each spouse of a bad relationship. However, in most cases the children still love both of their parents. Often they will not take sides. They feel torn. They even feel guilt-ridden and sometimes think the divorce is their fault. And yet because of pride, power struggles, and arguments between their parents, these children often go unnoticed. Understandably, they feel like pieces of property about to be divided.

A seven-year-old girl came up to her pastor after Sunday school and asked, "Pastor, can you please help me find a new home? I know that my parents don't really want me around the house anymore. All they do is argue and fight. And when they argue, they ask me to go to my room. I think they're fighting about me. I know that if I move away, they won't get a divorce, and they will love each other again. And they will be happy together again. I love them so much!" This is such a sad commentary. Yet her feelings were so real.

Church divorce mediation can put children back into their rightful seats of prominence. The ground rules of the one who founded our church are found in his words: "I am the good shepherd; I know my sheep and my sheep know me ... and I lay down my life for the sheep" (John 10:14, 15). Christ *cares* about the hurts of everyone, yet especially knows the helplessness of children. He even said, "Let the little children come to me" (Matt. 19:14). It *is* our responsibility to care for our children. This is something that we are not simply asked to do by Christ. He *commended* us to do this: "See that you do not look down on one of these little ones. For I tell you that their angels in heaven always see the face of my Father in heaven" (Matt. 18:10-11).

The Church and the Pastor

"Pride only breeds quarrels, but wisdom is found in those who take advice" (Prov. 13:10). The pastor who "waits" for the couple to come to her or him knows very well that such a strategy may be too late and realizes that "seeing the pastor" may be their last resort. Most clergy who have had this helpless experience know the frustrations of trying to patch things up. The couple comes back for a few more appointments (out of obligation) which often end up in shouting matches. Then, finally out of despair, they announce that the divorce hearing has been set for a certain date. They both want the divorce. The pastor can go through a lot of guilt and remorse as if it were his or her fault. Those who have been through this type of situation know that it is an extremely helpless and almost lonely feeling.

When Christian divorce mediation is available, it can be a valuable alternative for clergy. They can refer couples to Christian mediators with confidence.

The pastor can say, "Maybe I cannot help you, but I know of some alternatives for you to consider." Once a system of Christian divorce mediation is in place, clergy, counselors, and others can develop an effective referral system to use with families experiencing the pain of divorce.

THE CHURCH AND INTERVENTION

"Then the king said, 'Bring me a sword.' So they brought a sword for the king. He then gave an order: 'Cut the living child in two and give half to one and half to the other'" (1 Kings 3:16-28).

Disputes are biblical. We can turn the pages of our Bibles and find the people of God in quite a number of disputes. Two women claimed to be the mother of a certain baby. They went to King Solomon to solve their dispute. We know that Solomon came up with a rather drastic solution, but it worked! He solved the dispute with the wisdom that gave him a prominent place in history.

Those women asked Solomon to intervene. He acted not only as intervener, but as judge. It isn't the familiar court of law; nevertheless, we see an example of an ancient form of intervention.

In the New Testament, we find Jesus serving in quite a number of disputes as someone who could peacefully and tactfully intervene. Think of poor Martha complaining to Jesus about her sister, Mary. Immediately Jesus stopped Martha from giving Mary a good piece of her mind when he said, "Martha, Martha, you are worried and upset about many things, but only one thing is needed. Mary has chosen what is better, and it will not be taken away from her" (Luke 10:41-42).

Even among the disciples of Christ, there were disputes. The mother of James and John stirred up quite an argument when she requested of Jesus, "Grant that one of these two sons of mine may sit at your right and the other at your left in your kingdom" (Matt. 20:21). Of course the other 10 disciples were pretty irritated, and they let Jesus know! Jesus said to them, "Whoever wants to become great among you must be your servant, and whoever wants to be first must be your slave" (Matt. 20:26-67).

Even in his last hours on the cross, our Lord intervened when the two thieves on each side of him were arguing. He solved the dispute by saying to the one, "Today you will be with me in paradise" (Luke 23:43).

One pastor complained, "If I confront the couple who is going through this separation, I could very likely lose them as members of my church. So I have to be a little careful and wait until they make the choice to come to me first."

Christ shows us repeatedly that it is the business of the body of Christ to carry on his mission by plunging right into the business of life. If we are to be the church of Christ, we cannot be afraid to become involved in the ugly things that life sometimes brings. Many times, caring *is* very risky business.

Intervention is a large part of the Christian divorce mediation process. It requires the boldness to be willing to be involved in the lives of others. It requires, also, the boldness to be wrong.

Often, intervention can lead directly into the Christian divorce mediation process. A woman had gone through a divorce she didn't want and was experiencing severe depression. She went to a marriage counselor and said, "I feel empty, I feel lost, and I don't know how I'll function without my husband. He was the breadwinner, he took care of the books—he did everything! I know I cannot function on my own. It's a horrible feeling. I feel totally worthless to my family."

Unlike the secular society, the church has a magnificent treasury of knowledge, understanding, love, and forgiveness. Because of the grace and strength Christ gives us, we can meet problems face to face and accomplish what appears totally impossible. In the spirit of Isaiah we can say of the Lord, "He has sent me to bind up the brokenhearted." (That is what the transforming power of the love of our Lord Jesus Christ can accomplish in our lives!)

Yes, it is realistic to assume that the marriages that fail may not have the potential to once again become a "perfect union." Church divorce mediation is biblically supported by Paul when he writes, "If any of you has a dispute with another, dare he take it before the ungodly for judgment instead of before the saints? ... Do you not know that we will judge angels? How much more the things of this life! Therefore, if you have disputes about such matters, appoint as judges even men of little account in the church!" (1 Cor. 6:1, 3-4). The power of the gospel confronts us with the fact that we can "pick up the pieces" and move forward in confidence. The case of Randy and Sue clearly points out that anything is possible when Christ is placed in the center of a relationship. The mediator helped them see that their relationship could and would work with the power of the Lord Jesus Christ.

The Christian gospel admonishes us to try to assist people in any way we can. We should, to the best of our abilities, intervene before couples take their cases to the secular court system.

When mediation is available through the church, families can seek out a Christian mediator, deal with specific unresolved issues, and arrive at mutually acceptable and compatible agreements. It should be understood that

Christian mediation will be open to signs of the reconciliation from the couple since it *is* possible. The case of Randy and Sue shows it *can* happen.

However, at all times it should be kept in mind that the couple will work through their differences with guidance from a mediator by using peaceful means no matter how enormous the problems may appear. It is one method in which, regardless of the end result, families can move forward in hope and confidence by being constantly reminded that Christ, the mediator and Prince of Peace, is with them and helping them.

THE CHURCH AND THE PRESENCE OF CHRIST

"For where two or three come together in my name, there am I with them" (Matt. 18:20). The responsibilities of the body of Jesus Christ extend to every part of our lives. But, they all point to the actual presence of Jesus Christ in any given situation. Christ is present in every facet of our lives, trying to involve himself in our problems as well as being with us in good times.

It was Christ who said, "Whatever you did for one of the least of these brothers of mine, you did for me" (Matt. 25:40). Christ is telling us that some people and some situations do not seem very appealing. And yet it is these people and these situations that need our care and attention. We cannot ignore people with troubled marriages, or those already divorced, as though something was terribly wrong with them.

One concerned person recently said, "I really feel bad for my neighbors who are going through a divorce. I haven't said anything to them, because I don't feel it's really any of my business. I don't want to be called a meddler. Besides, what are the right things to say? I want to say that 'I care,' but I'm afraid that they will think I'm just being a nosy neighbor. How can I put my concern into the right words without sounding nosy?"

That is exactly the problem. We assume that when people are having problems we should stay out of their lives—it's none of our business. Again, this is totally contrary to everything Christ taught us. Thank goodness and praise God for the good Samaritans in our world who know there is risk in caring, and who are not afraid to take that risk.

The church mediation process claims its position as that of a caring body whose job it is to demonstrate Christ's grace and love. We are called to care for people on every level: physical, financial, spiritual, and so forth. This is our chance to say to families going through this type of painful trauma, "We care about you; we love you; we desperately want to help you if you will let us try."

Yes, Christian divorce mediation is biblical. As servants of Christ, we can readily understand how important our brothers and sisters are. It is time for church members to step forward and say, "Yes, I care; I want to be involved in your life. Let me walk through life with you, even if your life includes a troubled marriage or divorce."

CHAPTER SIX
What Happens in Mediation

We fear the courts, we fear lawyers, we fear the condemnation of the church, and now we begin to wonder if we shouldn't also fear mediation. This chapter explains what happens in mediation. It is presented in the hope that it will remove some of the anxiety a couple may experience as they approach the mediation process. Although each mediation is as unique as the mediator and the couple involved, mediation does lend itself to a process that can be described.

Do not be alarmed if your mediation does not follow the exact format proposed in this chapter. What happens in mediation is not ironclad—except in one respect: every attempt should be made to help the couple themselves resolve their differences openly and honestly.

THREE DIFFERENCES IN CHURCH MEDIATION

We recommend that any church providing mediation services review and adopt, in as many ways as possible, the rules of secular mediation. Various secular mediation organizations have adopted uniform rules. The Academy of Family Mediators of Eugene, Oregon, has established a set of rules for its mediators (address given in Appendix). There are, however, three differences the church mediation process should recognize and emphasize.

Reconciliation

The church, by its very endorsement of lifetime marital commitments, must be constantly alerted to signs of possible reconciliation between the spouses. Church mediators must be aware of this and must stand ready to suggest marriage counseling for the mediating couple at any point where reconciliation is posed as a possibility. The decision to dissolve or not to dissolve a marriage is not a proper issue for mediation, but church mediators should never assume that the decision to dissolve is a certainty until the couple has completed the mediation process. If counseling is sought, the mediation process should continue to work on short-term unresolved issues.

Forgiveness

The church is called to forgive and restore wholeness. The mediating couple must also be encouraged to forgive each other. Private confession of struggles and inadequacies should be encouraged, but not in the mediation process itself. Confession to a trusted pastor who is not serving as the mediator is recommended. The decision to forgive or not to forgive may not be a proper issue for secular mediation, but it can never be overlooked as central to the mission of church mediation. The couple needs to know that forgiveness is the work of the church, and that even if their marriage is concluded in divorce, divorce (certainly no less than any other sin) can be forgiven. The church mediator needs to be alert to moments when a word of forgiveness should be encouraged and spoken.

Prayer

The third difference between secular and church mediation is a visible one. Each session of the church mediation process should begin or conclude with prayer for the couple and the families that are affected. Secular mediation does not lend itself to this treatment, nor should it. The couple should also be assured that the mediator is praying for them by name during the mediation process.

Although there may be some discomfort on the part of a mediator or the couple to recognize and encourage reconciliation, forgiveness, and the open use of prayer, use of these accomplishes benefits that cannot be measured in terms of tangible outcomes. Instead, their presence actively shows a couple that the church is concerned about the wellness of the whole person—which includes not only the financial and emotional outcomes of a divorce, but the spiritual outcome as well.

THE FIRST MEETING

The first meeting between the mediator and the couple may take on an informal tone, but in that first meeting is an explicit assignment to set the parameters in which the mediation will work. The first meeting is critical, not so much in deciding the issues, but in deciding and understanding the framework in which the mediation process will work.

Confidentiality

In the first session, the mediator will emphasize the need for confidentiality. No discussion should take place with relatives, friends, coworkers, or other professional people without the prior agreement of the mediator and couple. Outside influences can cloud issues and present confusion for a mediating couple. What happens in mediation must be between the couple and the mediator alone in order to assure its success.

The couple should also be assured—and agree in writing—that the mediator will not be called upon to testify in court. Conversations and sessions between the mediator and the couple will be confidential. The cloak of confidentiality leads the couple to be open to expressing doubts and struggles, knowing that those statements will not be used in any later court hearing.

To ensure the success of mediation, the couple also agrees that they will not speak to the mediator individually. In that respect, mediation is not like therapy, where a counselor may meet with marital partners together and separately. Mediation, after all, is the direct effort to get the couple to communicate and solve problems. Individual meetings with the mediator would only add confusion and distrust to that unique setting in which mediation works.

Responsibility for payment of mediation

Mediation involves professional people; an expense is involved to provide this service. In the first session, the couple needs to come to some agreement with the mediator about the cost. In secular mediation, there typically are fees for the mediator. Included in that fee is the cost of the mediation center. In addition, the husband and wife would each be responsible for hiring their own attorney prior to the conclusion of the mediation process. Christian mediation would likely follow a similar plan.

In all likelihood, the church providing the mediation will propose a sliding fee scale for the payment of fees.

The payment of a nominal amount should be required of all participating in the mediation process, however. Although the payment of a fee may seem cruel or even unnecessary in certain instances, experience shows that couples who are paying for services are more likely to follow the recommendations that result.

Time requirements

It is imperative that a couple come to some realization about the time that is needed to mediate their marital dissolution. Couples may enter mediation with the illusion that everything will be completed after one or two meetings. The average mediation may take four to twelve sessions, depending on the issues that need to be addressed. Any couple involved in church mediation should be aware that they will be involved in at least four sessions of mediation.

The couple will need to establish a time frame in which to work. Mediation should be regular and consistent. Each session should be approximately one to two hours and should be weekly. During the first session, the mediator and the couple should establish a working schedule for all successive meetings.

Openness and honesty in fact finding

The couple should be assured that openness and honesty are paramount in the mediation process. Hiding of information and assets will only make the process encumbered and more difficult. The need for openness cannot be stressed enough and both parties should agree in the first meeting to work from that premise.

Defining the process

To take the mystery out of mediation, the mediator in the first session will define the process of mediation for the couple and explain what will happen in successive sessions. The church mediator will also point out the three distinct differences between church mediation and secular mediation.

The mediator may briefly explain that successive sessions will involve: fact finding in issues involving the children, spouses, and marital and nonmarital property; points of agreement and disagreement, compromise, and options; settlement; review of that settlement and its implementation.

Defining impasse

The mediator must point out that not all mediation is successful, and certain conditions will set forth an impasse in the sessions. If there is an unwillingness to provide needed information, an unwillingness to pay fees, a breach in confidentiality, or a lack of agreement, an impasse will exist.

At that point, it is hoped that the mediator, with the agreement of the couple, can discontinue the mediation sessions. The mediator must also emphasize that people who wish to mediate their differences, and who come to a mediator with that hope, are likely to be successful in coming to a resolution of differences.

Immediate concerns

Immediate concerns regarding the children must be handled at the first session. A schedule for the children to be with each parent should be established for the first week until the couple meets with the mediator again. Husband and wife should also agree not to sell or dispose of any assets.

Signing an agreement to mediate

The agreement to mediate contains all the rules by which mediation proceeds. By signing such an agreement, the couple openly and freely agrees that they will abide by the rules of mediation and that they will actively attempt to resolve their differences in that manner. The signing should be delayed until the second meeting so the couple can think it over.

Setting the tone for the second meeting

The couple should be asked to bring any counseling information they may have to the second session so that the issue of reconciliation can be reviewed. The mediator again should emphasize that it is not the role of the mediator to decide whether the marriage should be dissolved, but it is the role of the mediator as a Christian to seek information that assures the couple that they have sought available help and are at a point where they wish to proceed to end the marriage in a peaceful way.

The close of the first session should end in prayer and in a friendly, reassuring way.

THE SECOND MEETING

The second meeting is different from those in secular mediation. It cannot be emphasized enough that mediation is not a counseling session, but at the second meeting between the husband and wife, the church-trained mediator should openly discuss any marital counseling the couple has sought.

Review of the counseling effort

A review of the counseling effort should be made, not to pass judgment on the counseling itself or the decision of the couple to dissolve their marriage, but to open avenues for discussion between the couple. Do they believe any more counseling would be worth considering? Do they believe their marriage is irreconcilable? Do they still have questions whether they should continue to remain married? Do they wonder whether their marriage can be saved? Do they need counseling to help them bring closure to their marriage (marital termination counseling may be available)?

1) If both husband and wife are uncertain of the decision to terminate the marriage, the mediator should suggest counseling for the couple. The mediator should not be the counselor. The mediation should be continued during the counseling process in order to protect the parties and to consider options for the future.

2) If either the husband or the wife believes an inadequate counseling effort has been made, the mediator should again suggest counseling for the couple. The mediator should explain to the couple that mediation is most successful when both husband and wife believe the marriage should be ended. Although it is not often that both parties agree on the dissolution of the marriage bond at the same time, additional follow-up marital counseling may help in resolving that critical issue. The couple should be referred to a marriage counselor who is supportive of the mediation process. The mediation should continue as a safe environment to consider future options.

3) If both husband and wife believe the marriage should be terminated, and have assured themselves that an adequate counseling and therapy effort has been made, the mediation process should continue without referral. It must be emphasized that what may appear to be adequate in some instances may not be in others. The mediator should strongly suggest counseling, especially in

instances where little or no counseling has occurred, but should also be willing to abide by the desires of the couple. Mediation, after all, is for the couple themselves. The mediator should not be a roadblock, but a facilitator of the peaceful resolution of differences.

Even though the couple has decided the marriage should be ended, the mediator should explain that while the decision to divorce is helpful for the successful continuation of the mediation process, it is not an irreversible decision. If at any time during the mediation process, either husband or wife has reservations about that decision, the mediator should suggest and encourage counseling.

Unlike the secular model, church mediation, by its very nature, encourages the marital reconciliation of the couple, as inconvenient and cumbersome as it may seem at times. It would be easier for the mediator not to have to look for those moments when a word of reconciliation or a word suggesting marital counseling could be spoken, but in order to remain faithful to the goal of marriage as a lifetime commitment, the church approaches the mediation process from this uniquely different stance.

If the couple wants to continue with mediation, the agreement to mediate should be signed. Then the mediator should offer prayer for the couple and instruct them to bring information about the children to the third meeting. They should bring medical information, school information, and information about the children's abilities, special needs, religious instruction, basic needs, and their relationships with each parent, siblings, and with significant relatives. The parents should also be prepared to discuss their ability to parent in terms of time, concern, and financial resources.

The mediator should also help resolve any immediate concerns the couple has about the children.

THE THIRD MEETING

If the couple has children, the third meeting concerns their welfare. This session is a fact-finding session, and the couple should be reassured that no decisions regarding the residence of the children or the amount of support that will be paid is to be decided at this time, unless the couple desires that be done. The couple may need to be reminded that mediation is not a fast process but a thorough one.

Needs of each child

The needs of each child should be discussed separately. The couple should be encouraged to discuss and exchange any medical information about each child. The health of a child can present major obstacles for a parent in residence, and the parents should discuss how medical concerns will be resolved. Medical information should be made available for this session.

The schooling and education of each child is likewise a critical subject—something too often ignored in a fast-paced adversarial divorce. Mediation encourages openness and gives the couple the freedom and time to talk about their children's education needs. School records should be available for this session.

In this session each parent should talk about his or her relationship with each child, and what can be done to continue to foster a closeness between parent and child. In some instances the mediator may suggest family counseling so the child and parents can work through any difficulties that arise.

Each child has different abilities and interests, and the parents should be encouraged to talk about each child's talents. Possibly a child has certain abilities or skills that will require additional fostering. Even though the parents are divorcing and are occupied with their concerns, the children still have needs that must be met. Too often the children are left in the shambles, and their life-style is significantly changed after divorce. Mediation encourages the parents to seek ways of fulfilling each child's needs.

The religious upbringing of the child is not only an appropriate subject to be discussed, but a critical concern for church mediation. The parents should discuss a plan that includes how the religious education of the children will continue or be resumed. Especially if a child is not with the same parent each weekend, the continuity of the religious instruction may be jeopardized. The parents should be encouraged to discuss ways to prevent upheaval in the religious life of the child.

The relationships a child has with siblings or other significant relatives (grandparents being the most likely), and how those relationships can be maintained and encouraged after a divorce should be discussed as well.

The clothing, shelter, and food needs of each child must be discussed. A budget for each child should be prepared and each parent should realistically look at the expense of raising each child. Include any special education expenses, camping, or extracurricular activities.

Needs of the children as a family unit

Most jurisdictions discourage the splitting up of children when a divorce occurs. It is necessary to look not only at the needs of the children individually, but also as a family unit. How the children relate to each other, to each parent, and to other relatives and friends, is significant.

The parents should be prepared to discuss how a family unit can be maintained with the least amount of chaos or emotional trauma for the children. They are the innocent ones.

Parental abilities to fill needs

After looking at the needs of each child and the relationship of that child to a family unit, each parent should be prepared to express how he or she would meet the needs of the children in terms of time, emotional concern, and financial demands.

The mediator should emphasize that church mediation does not recognize a gender preference or "early years with the mother" doctrine. What is important is to determine how each parent can best meet the needs of the children. It is also critical that parents make the decisions rather than the children, although older children can be involved in planning schedules.

Parental desires

Although no permanent residency or support questions should be resolved at this session so that open and honest fact finding is not hindered, each parent may wish to express his or her personal desires for the children, and how he or she would see the needs of the children best met.

The third mediation session is an involved one and is of the greatest concern. If additional time is necessary, a fourth and even fifth session can be devoted to the children. It is also advisable to contact an advisory attorney at this point if questions arise about the laws concerning support and custodial arrangements for children.

The third session should end with a prayer in which the children are named and prayed for specifically. Any special needs that a child may have should be mentioned in prayer.

The Fourth Meeting

Prior to the fourth meeting, the mediator should ask the couple to update all of their housing, education, medical, and other major costs. This would include a detailed budget of current and anticipated expenditures and income.

The fourth meeting is devoted to fact finding about each spouse. The mediator, in order to encourage open and honest discussion, should emphasize that this session is structured to fact finding only. No decisions are expected or demanded of the couple at this point regarding the support and residence of each spouse.

Needs of the spouse

Some mediators at this point ask each spouse to prepare a budget for the other. Although this may cause some hesitancy, it is a good exercise in learning about the other. It also takes the emphasis away from "my" wants and desires. Other mediators may simply ask that each spouse prepare his or her own budget.

Each partner should be prepared to talk about his or her housing requirements, employment history and potential, the amount of money necessary to live, and his or her emotional, physical, and spiritual needs. Options should be discussed.

Earnings and potential

Each partner must bring current earnings statements to this session of mediation, along with an employment history and tax returns for the preceding five years. The earnings statements should show all deductions from gross pay. In addition, information often not shown on a wage statement such as insurance, pension, vacation, overtime, and sick leave benefits, should be made accessible.

If a spouse is self-employed or employed by a business in which he or she has a major interest, current income balance sheets should be made available as well as all supporting schedules of assets and depreciation.

Spousal maintenance needs

From the information given concerning earnings, each spouse should be prepared to talk about his or her financial needs and whether additional support is necessary and reasonable. Although spousal maintenance (commonly called alimony) usually raises concern, in many instances where one of the spouses is underemployed and the potential to earn is not significant, maintenance should be discussed.

The fourth session should end with specific prayer for each of the partners in the marriage.

THE FIFTH MEETING

Prior to the fifth meeting, the mediator should advise the couple to locate all information concerning property they own or have brought into the marriage. The couple will need to locate all information concerning *real* property (homes, lake property, or other land) and personal property (bank accounts, stocks and bonds, annuities, pensions, life insurance policies, vehicles, boats, aircraft, business property, household items, and any other property that is owned by either the husband or wife). Local laws may differ and the following definitions are general in nature.

Marital assets

Marital assets are those that have been acquired during the marriage. Marital assets are considered to be the property of both husband and wife, although some of those assets may have been acquired through the earnings of only one spouse. The marital assets and their values, including their appreciated values, should be determined.

Although appraisals may be expensive, certain property lends itself to appraisals. Pensions and real property need expert valuations. Certain motor vehicles and business property should also be appraised, unless the couple can agree on value figures that are acceptable to them. It is always more difficult to decide what to do when all the facts are not available. A mediator should recommend a complete appraisal.

The couple may wish to value the assets at the time of separation or any date they find mutually acceptable.

Marital debts

Marital debts are those incurred during the marriage for marital or normal household expenses. Those debts should include debts on real property (mortgages), consumer debts on cars, charge accounts, and other promissory notes. Complete and thorough information is necessary in order to evaluate the amount of debt the couple has.

Nonmarital assets

Nonmarital assets are those assets that were owned prior to marriage or acquired as a gift or inheritance from someone other than the spouse during the marriage. A careful tracing of those assets should be made. They may be real property or personal property and the value of any such assets should be ascertained either by the couple or an independent appraiser.

Nonmarital debts

Nonmarital debts are those debts that were incurred prior to marriage (e.g., unpaid college loans) or were acquired against nonmarital assets. Debt that is exclusively nonfamilial in nature and beyond normal and reasonable living should also be considered as nonmarital debt.

If the couple is unable to obtain all the information concerning assets and debts, additional mediation sessions should be devoted to this process to insure complete and accurate information. It is good stewardship to carefully look at the value of assets and how those assets should be divided.

This session should end in prayer that possessions will not become so important that the welfare of children or either of the spouses is overlooked.

THE SIXTH MEETING

The sixth meeting in mediation is critical. For the first time the couple will be asked to define areas of disagreement and agreement. The mediator should emphasize the areas of agreement, while always encouraging and working toward solutions and options in areas of disagreement. At this session, it is important to simply define areas of agreement and disagreement. Demanding settlement or strongly suggesting settlement may leave the couple feeling pressured and frustrated. Many times negotiations fail over minor differences.

The children

The parents will be asked to determine the parental exchange of the children, support for the children, involvement of each parent in the upbringing of the children, insurance coverage, and the religious, educational, and medical concerns of each child.

The plan for the children should be comprehensive and thorough. Many parents who complete mediation have actively thought out and sought out solid plans of action for their parenting involvement—something all couples could benefit from doing.

The spouse

Each spouse should understand the needs of the other spouse. Mediation sets a tone for thinking of the needs of the other person: future employment opportunities and needs, residential needs, support needs, and medical insurance needs.

The couple, from the information gathered, should be able to present a well-defined plan for each spouse.

Division of property and payment of debts

The couple should also be able to discuss their desires for the division of real and personal property, both marital and nonmarital, and for the payment of debts. Points of agreement should be encouraged, and points of disagreement should be noted for the follow-up session.

Session six should end in prayer and thanksgiving for the couple—that they have brought their concerns to mediation in an effort to peacefully resolve differences.

The Seventh Meeting

Any points of disagreement should be addressed in this session and the mediator should be ready to suggest compromise, alternatives, or other options. The mediator should only suggest and not force or compel a response from the couple. It is critical that the couple mutually arrive at a settlement they can live with.

If disagreement exists on several issues, an additional session should be scheduled. It is important for the couple to realize that settlement is possible, and the fact that they are meeting to discuss that settlement continues to be a positive sign.

THE EIGHTH MEETING

Once an agreement has been reached on all issues, a session to discuss the final settlement should be scheduled. Normally a mediator will have made charts on which the agreements have been listed. The couple will orally agree to the terms, and any modifications can be made.

THE NINTH MEETING

Review of the memorandum of agreement, as drafted by the mediator, is usually the final step in secular mediation. The couple meets to review the document, and although they do not sign the document, it is important for both husband and wife to read the agreement and orally agree to its content. At that point the couple will decide who to hire as an attorney to review the agreement and represent them in court. Separate attorneys should be chosen, but only one attorney may be asked to draft the legal documents necessary to conclude the dissolution in the courts of law. The other attorney simply reviews the documents. Attorneys chosen should be supportive of the mediation process.

THE TENTH MEETING

A service of forgiveness should be used in the final session of mediation to bring closure to the relationship. The service of forgiveness may occur after the divorce has been finalized in the courts. It may involve the children and other close friends if the couple desires. The service of forgiveness does not condone divorce, but instead offers the forgiveness of Christ for sin in our human lives. The service should be one of praise and thanksgiving for the peaceful resolution of marital differences. It should include specific prayers for the couple as they begin their separate lives, and for the children of the marriage.

Following this service of forgiveness, if the couple desires, an announcement in the congregation's bulletin may include words such as, _____ and _____ (names of couple) have mediated their marital differences through _____ (name of the church). They have chosen to end their marital relationship, and ask for the forgiveness, prayer, and love of the congregation as they lead their separate lives.

CHAPTER SEVEN
Establishing a Ministry of Conflict Resolution

Statistics, which show that one in every two marriages end in divorce, tell us that the family of today is in a severe crisis. This book presented four case histories in which families were going through the pain of severe problems and separations. Yet these are only four couples out of thousands each year who either divorce or who are contemplating divorce. Only one of these four couples, Randy and Sue, preserved their marriage. The other three could have used Christian divorce mediation for peacemaking and resolving various issues.

While the restoration of the marriage can always be a hope in the mediation process, most couples will probably not be reconciled. However, mediation will help all those couples walk through the steps leading to divorce with the ultimate goal of peacefully making decisions about issues affecting both of them—before any legal action is taken. Mediation is organized to help a couple resolve their differences themselves.

In contrast, counseling is designed to guide and assist the couple in working on their relationship, communication skills, and emotional issues. Since Christian divorce mediation opens up communication, it can lead the couple to consider seeing a counselor, perhaps at the same time as the mediation. Counseling can help couples who want to reconcile their differences and also those who wish to end their marriage.

In contrast to secular mediation, Christian divorce mediation encourages the peaceful resolving of differences within the family structure by reminding the couple of the grace and forgiveness available through Jesus Christ. Christian divorce mediation assists a couple in deciding for themselves what is right, just, and good.

This book is meant to encourage congregations, church agencies, and other groups to become familiar with Christian divorce mediation and to consider establishing such a program. It should be approached as an integral part of the life of the congregation. While divorce is a sensitive issue, the church has responsibility to deal with it. In a wedding service, some congregations include a prayer which says, "use us [the congregation] to support their [the couple's] life together" (*Lutheran Book of Worship,* p. 204).

It should be clarified that setting up a Christian divorce mediation process does not mean that the church is condoning divorce. However, we cannot deny the intense reality of divorce, and we certainly cannot close our eyes to the realities that exist in our lives day after day.

The subject should be approached openly, honestly, and sensitively. A great deal of dialog should be encouraged. The congregation considering this process should also have no hesitation to call on various resource people who are knowledgeable in the areas of divorce and mediation: trained mediators, attorneys, pastors, medical professionals, and others whose professions are in human services or law.

As the body of Jesus Christ, we should also acknowledge that we have one of the most valuable resources available to humankind, the Bible. Yes, Christian divorce mediation is biblical. Bible studies can be established as a part of an adult education program. Studying the Bible passages discussed at the close of Chapter 4 and in Chapter 5 is one way to begin. Of course, it should be readily acknowledged that the Bible is such an inexhaustible supply of wisdom that many passages could be used. Each congregation can create its own study depending on the needs, questions, and concerns of its members.

After careful study and deliberation, through dialog and Bible study, the concept of Christian divorce mediation can be presented to the congregation. This could be done in the form of an open meeting in order to formalize the proposal to organize a board to manage the project. It is very possible that this will require a change in the local church constitution, bylaws, or governing documents. Carefully examine those documents in order to determine the legal number of votes needed and steps to follow to accomplish your goals.

It is also realistic to assume that this will not be popular in some congregations. The mere mention of the word *divorce* ruffles some feathers. However, this should not prevent the subject from being pursued. Some awareness will be created and a real need will be discussed. This will encourage open dialog in a much neglected area which should be uppermost in the mission of the church of Jesus Christ.

The board of mediation

After the concept of Christian divorce mediation has been approved by the congregation, a board of mediation should be established. The characteristics and responsibilities of this board include the following:

1) Membership should be limited to no more than seven and no less than four members.

2) Members of the board should be active members of the congregation. They should be available for consultation as needed. Ideally, the pastor and a person from the legal profession should at all times be advisory members of this board.

3) The board's central responsibility is to find, screen, and interview potential mediators, eventually hiring one or more as needed and arranging for training. The board should meet regularly with a trained mediator during this process in order to maintain current standards of mediation, maintain familiarity with changing divorce laws, and review mediation policies.

4) Make plans for the training of the mediator(s). (pp. 128-130.)

5) The board should establish policies, oversee, and serve as advisors to the mediator(s). However, the board should not be actively involved in the cases. This would impair confidentiality for the families taking part in the mediation process.

6) Establish guidelines for payment of the mediator(s). Keep in mind that mediators are professionals and are performing a professional service.

This board should be seen as an integral part of the life and mission of the congregation. It is very important for the board to maintain a relatively high profile in the congregation for the purpose of familiarizing every member with this relatively new concept.

In the beginning stages, the congregation may see fit to place this board under the direction of another committee or board of the congregation. For example, if the congregation has a board of family life and growth, mediation could be an extension of that.

Beginning a Mediation Program

The board of mediation should seek out resource people to serve as mediator(s). While many persons in each congregation could be qualified to mediate, it is extremely important that members *not* be asked to serve as mediators in their own congregations. Couples may feel uncomfortable and inhibited with someone they know. Also, there is the possibility that the mediator could have a tendency to prejudge a situation.

It is important that the guidelines be explicit for being a mediator. There should be an accreditation process, perhaps established by the board, but preferably developed by a number of congregations working together. It should be stressed that while there are many well-intentioned people in our congregations who think they would be good mediators, the training and education of the persons selected are extremely important. Because of skills unique to mediation, applicants should have previous professional training in the ministry, family counseling, law, or mediation fields. In addition to these professional skills, there should be a solid training program offered. Several congregations or a regional group might sponsor such training. It might also be offered through educational settings—perhaps seminaries eventually.

The training event should be planned and conducted by people who have experience in mediation and who are

knowledgeable in fields directly related to Christian divorce mediation. The following are some elements that need to be included in the training:
1. Orientation
2. Description of Christian divorce mediation and information about and the history of mediation in general
3. Determination of the best settings for Christian divorce mediation
4. Defining the mediation process; what happens in the sessions
5. The role and responsibility of the mediator
6. Materials needed to acquire information from couples
7. Skills and knowledge needed by mediators
8. Hypothetical cases for group discussion
9. The congregation and Christian divorce mediation
10. The personal involvement and commitment of the mediator
11. The role of attorneys
12. Remuneration for services given
13. Drafting the settlement agreement
14. The possibility of further counseling and/or reconciliation

Previous experience in the human service or legal professions is necessary. For example, a family counselor will have many of the skills necessary for mediation. While mediation is not counseling, knowledge of counseling skills and techniques is very important in many of the stages of this process. For instance, Randy and Sue's mediator was a person who was obviously familiar with counseling skills and also had an understanding of family problems, symptoms, and tensions. A mediator who is from the legal profession possesses extensive knowledge of divorce laws, and procedures of divorce settlements and agreements. Such a person has skills which will prove valuable in many of the stages of Christian divorce mediation.

The professional nature of mediation *has* to be protected. In order to maintain this degree of professionalism, mediators should be certified through a church certification process. A couple will be inclined to have a higher trust level when they know that the mediator is indeed qualified to handle the delicate problems being experienced in their marriage and family. We live in a day and age when people expect professionalism in areas that affect their future well-being.

Relying on the Holy Spirit

Because this is Christian divorce mediation, we have to keep in mind that we are relying on the Holy Spirit of Christ at all times. The mediator should be involved in prayer for and with the couple at all stages of the process. The mediator should remind the couple that Christ wants to be actively involved in our lives. So often when a couple seeks help, solutions seem next to impossible. When couples choose to participate in Christian divorce mediation, they soon learn the key role that prayer plays. This is so important since, as Christians, we believe anything is possible when we invite the power of the Spirit of Jesus Christ into our lives.

Defining the process

The mediator needs to define Christian divorce mediation to the couple. Mediation seeks to find workable answers for various differences and conflicts by concentrating on positives rather than negatives. Mediation will "walk through" the problem areas but will not deal with them the way counseling does. Randy and Sue sought the help of the mediator to work out their differences in order to peacefully make decisions in areas of conflict. However, when counseling was seen as an option to working out their problems on a deeper level, the mediator stepped back by making a referral to their pastor for counseling. The hope is that this will happen often when Christian divorce mediation is utilized.

The commitment of time

After the process of mediation has been defined, the couple should be made aware of the commitment of time they are making. Christian divorce mediation can be a time-consuming process. The couple has to be willing to follow this process through to its completion. It is imperative to get a commitment from the couple by having them sign a document stating they will complete the mediation process. This document is valuable in case tempers flare, complacency sets in, or the couple just wants to "get it over with once and for all." Because mediation involves the professional services of the mediator, the necessity of remuneration has to be discussed. Payment of a fee increases the family's commitment to the mediation process. It also is another reminder to the family of the professional nature of Christian divorce mediation.

Setting goals

While the time needed varies, it is important that the mediator establish a schedule with the family. Each couple has different problem areas. The mediator should help point them out and set goals with the couple. The mediator should always give an estimate of the time each of these areas could take.

Trust

Because of the issue of confidentiality, couples may be hesitant to employ the services of a stranger. A good trust level is important to the mediation process. It is extremely important that the mediator advise and receive the consent of the parties that he or she will not be asked to testify in any court proceedings unless both parties agree. The ideal situation would be that this process not end up in the courts; that the couple would become motivated to work on saving their marriage. The mediator should make a commitment to watch for and encourage signs of reconciliation. When there are such signs, the mediation process may lead the couple back to counseling.

Knowledge the Mediator Should Possess

Laws

Because the laws in each of the 50 states vary, mediators need to possess at least a limited working knowledge of the divorce laws in the state in which they are practicing. Familiarity with the laws can give guidance to the mediator regarding the rights of each parent, schedules for being with the children, guidelines for child support payments, and obligations of each parent to the children. Knowledge of these laws can help give the mediator credibility with the couple.

Trends

The mediator should be knowledgeable about current trends in mediation, conflict management, and communication skills. Regarding the latter, there are certain conversational and listening techniques that are valuable to the process of mediation. Mediation is not counseling, but various counseling techniques can be valuable in helping a couple make decisions.

Children

Probably the most painful aspect of divorce is that children are the innocent victims. In divorce cases, the rights and needs of children often go unnoticed. Mediation gives the needs of the children a prominent position in the decision making of the parents. Because there are concerns, needs, and feelings on the part of the children, it is crucially important that the parents talk with their children about what is happening (the children do not usually attend the sessions, however). If the children are not involved as decisions are made, it is highly possible that problems can result at a later time. Children go through feelings of guilt, thinking they caused the divorce. They can go through feelings of uselessness, thinking their parents don't love them anymore. They can experience self-consciousness among their peers, thinking they are different from everyone else because they will no longer be a "complete" family. They may feel "branded." A child can very likely be angry with his or her parents.

Mary, whose parents were divorcing, told her pastor, "I think my parents are two of the most cruel people I know. Not once did they ask me what I thought of what they were doing. Not once did they think I was old enough [she was 15] to understand. I hate my mother. I hate my father. I would just like to run away and get away from my parents. They don't even give a rip about my feelings." Since Mary was not involved in her parents' decision making, her potential problems are obvious to a perceptive person.

In dealing with families, counselors have identified various symptoms that children develop which indicate a variety of potential problems:

1) Withdrawing from people. Often a child will become very quiet and shut himself or herself off from everyone. Timmy was an only child. At the age of seven, his parents divorced. Throughout the entire ordeal of court hearings and then the divorce itself, Timmy became more and more withdrawn. His mother, who became the custodial parent, tried to explain the reasons for the divorce. But each time she tried to talk to him, he would walk to his room, close the door, and not come out for several hours. Finally Timmy's mother brought him to a counselor. After several sessions, Timmy told his mother he resented his parents for not asking him what he thought about the divorce or what he felt his rights were, and for not giving him a chance to be a part of the family's decision making.

2) Falling grades in school. The child may eventually lose interest in things that were once important. Life can become totally meaningless for the child. After all, the child's entire world is falling apart.

3) Seeking "lower company." Particularly in the case of teenagers, they will seek different friends as a form of rebellion. Jane was a 15-year-old girl who was ambitious in school, well-liked by her peers, and who loved her parents very much. After her parents divorced, she became quite cynical and moody. Eventually she started running around with the wrong crowd, stayed out late, avoided her old circle of friends, and began using alcohol and drugs. Her mother waited up late one night for her daughter to come home. When Jane finally came home at three o'clock that morning, her mother realized Jane was drunk. She tried to talk to Jane, but she couldn't because Jane was drunk. Her mother was grief-stricken. The next day, her

mother went to the school counselor. Eventually counseling was started between Jane and her mother. After several weeks, her father was asked to participate in the counseling. Through this process, once again, it was discovered that Jane had an intense resentment toward her parents for not consulting her, for not involving her in their decision making in regard to the divorce.

These are just a few of the symptoms to be aware of regarding children. But regardless of the outcome of the mediation, the important fact to remember is that children have a part in the decision making of the family. They have the right, as integral parts of the family, to voice their concerns, objections, and their needs. Yet parents are the ones who must make the final decisions.

Peacemaking

Finally, before beginning the mediation the mediator should keep in mind the rules established for peacemaking and have an understanding of the Christian hope for reconciliation. Yes, that is the ultimate hope since all things, *all things,* are possible because of Christ. Christ himself intervenes in our lives by saying in effect, "I have come into your lives because I love you and I care about you. Let me help you. I have never left you in bad times. Turn to me so I can help you have the life God intended for you!"

PREMARRIAGE AGREEMENT

Actually, mediation begins the minute a prospective bride and groom announce their engagement to the pastor. It is common practice for the pastor to request or require that the couple come in for several premarital guidance sessions. Many couples walk into marriage with blinders on. William Hulme, in his book *The Pastoral Care of Families,* maintains that "young couples, even if they are aware of problems, are looking to marriage itself as the answer to them all" (Abingdon Press, 1962). Premarital guidance sessions help the couple see things realistically.

When the pastor and couple have met with one another for several sessions, there should be a commitment made between them. First, "When the pastor decides that he should go ahead and marry the couple, his invitation to return to him whenever the couple has need may be the most important words he speaks" (Hulme, 1962). After that invitation, marriage crisis counseling should be discussed. There should be a commitment (verbal and signed) between the pastor and the couple, that if there are problems that could lead to possible alienation and divorce, the couple will first seek mediation through the system offered by the church. Provided in the appendix of this book is a document entitled "Premarriage Agreement." It states that "prior to seeking legal recourse to terminate our marriage, . . . we agree that we shall in good faith first seek out the intervention of a Christian church participating in mediation for marriages." This may seem to be somewhat depressing to a couple who can only see happy days ahead. However, it is interesting to note that of couples who were asked if they would sign this agreement, almost 100 percent replied that they would. However, the story was much different when couples who had been married for several years were asked to sign the same document. We can draw our own conclusions from that!

While mediation has not been systematically tried in the church up to this point, we only have to think of the many who have been married in our churches with apparently bright futures ahead of them, only to see their names appear in the "Marriage Dissolution" section of the local newspaper a few years later. Again the question has to be asked, If the church takes the responsibility to marry people, shouldn't the church be equally involved in crisis situations which sometimes lead to marriage dissolution?

THE CHURCH GETS INVOLVED

For years, the church has been kept in the dark regarding the failure of marriages. Occasionally a couple will come to the pastor's office with problems that lead to divorce. But very often it will be too late at that point for the pastor to guide the couple into a marital reconciliation. The next step will be for the couple to seek the help of attorneys to represent them in court.

Christian divorce mediation can be a step in between the session with the pastor and the final court appearance ending their marriage. The couple wants the pastor to intervene on their behalf. But often the results are not what the couple expects from this crisis intervention. It can sometimes lead to a temporary Band-aid approach, with the symptoms gradually occurring again over a period of time.

Christian divorce mediation can be an effective referral system for pastors, attorneys, marriage counselors, psychologists, social workers, and doctors. The court doesn't have to be the next step anymore. If mediation leads to reconciliation of the marriage, the court doesn't have to go the final step either. In some cases marriages can be restored when the couple is open to explore reconciliation, because all things are possible with God. Remember that it was Christ who said, "I came that they may have life, and have it abundantly!"

Whatever the outcome, the church, in the name of Christ, must stand willing to help each couple mediate their differences in a peaceful, resolving way, and to love, forgive, and embrace them as they work out their future—a future that may include a divorce.

"For there is one God, and one mediator between God and men, the man Christ Jesus. . . . I want men everywhere to lift up holy hands in prayer, without anger or disputing" (1 Tim. 2:5,8).

Appendix

PREMARRIAGE AGREEMENT

I

We believe in the holiness and sacredness of marriage, and we desire that our commitment to each other will last a lifetime. We want to express that commitment to each other on the _____ day of _____ , 19 _____ .

II

We have specifically asked to be married at _____ (name of church) with address of _____ , City of _____ , State of _____ . We understand that we will be married in a Christian ceremony of marriage.

III

We recognize that we could choose to be married before an official acting on the part of the State of _____ , solely, but we have specifically chosen not only to give our marriage a legal status, but a spiritual one as well by declaring before the Christian community our desire to live as husband and wife.

IV

We also recognize that the legal status of our marriage may be terminated by divorce in the courts of law, but because we have specifically chosen a spiritual status for our marriage as well, we therefore agree, before the Christian community and to each other, that prior to seeking legal recourse to terminate our marriage (unless intervention of law enforcement shall be necessary because of physical abuse), we agree that we shall in good faith first seek out the intervention of a Christian church participating in mediation for marriages.

V

We understand that such a program is designed specifically to help us address the reconciliation of the relationship, but if such is not a workable solution to our struggles, then to mediate such issues as the support, care, nurturing, and residence of minor children, the support and care of each spouse, the division of marital and nonmarital property, and such other issues as the couple and the mediator agree are appropriate.

VI

We also understand that should mediation not be successful in resolving our differences, we may also, at our option, request an arbitrator appointed through such mediation program, to render a binding decision for us.

VII

We willingly agree to this plan of action, and agree to utilize and ask for mediation services of the church as soon as problems arise in our marriage.

VIII

We acknowledge and are thankful that the church stands willing to intervene on our behalf and does so out of concern for our welfare and the welfare of any children we may have, and that such authority is based on Matthew 18:15-35, 19:1-5; and 1 Corinthians 6:1-7 and 7:1-24.

IX

We ask that our vows sustain us and bless us in the years to come, and that in the event mediation of marital disputes becomes necessary, that faithful and loving mediators will provide the support, love, and prayer needed to help us resolve our differences peacefully.

X

We understand that this agreement shall be binding if our marriage is concluded and not otherwise.

XI

We have signed this agreement as a pledge of our commitment to each other and to the Christian community that we will work towards lifetime fulfillment of our marriage vows.

IN TESTIMONY WHEREOF, we have signed our names this ____ day of _____ , 19 ____ .

_____

_____

IN WITNESS WHEREOF, we have signed our names as witnesses that the above-named parties did willingly and with full knowledge sign the same, and were under no duress or undue influence. (Preferably the best man and maid-of-honor, if of legal age, will sign this agreement as witnesses prior to the day of the wedding.)

_____

_____

_____
Approved: Pastor

NOTE: This agreement must be signed prior to the wedding day.

Legal Precedent

After the decision in *Avitzur v. Avitzur,* 58 NY 2d 108, 459 NYS 2d 572, 446 NE 2d 136, there is reason to believe that the premarriage agreement found in this appendix may be upheld with the full force of law. An Orthodox Jewish couple, married in the Orthodox Jewish tradition, entered into an agreement prior to their marriage that stated that either party would appear before a religious tribunal upon request of the other.

The wife requested her husband to appear before the "Beth Din." The husband refused. At issue is the enforceability of a document known as a Ketubah, which was entered into as part of a religious ceremony. Although the husband obtained a civil divorce, the wife was not considered divorced and could not remarry without a Jewish divorce decree known as a "Get." In order to obtain that decree, both the husband and wife had to appear before a rabbinical tribunal having authority to advise and pass upon matters of traditional Jewish law.

The court ruled that an agreement to refer a matter concerning marriage to arbitration suffers no inherent invalidity and that duly executed antenuptial agreements, which parties agree to in advance of marriage, are valid and enforceable.

Additional Referral Information

If no mediation service is available through your church, either on a local, district, or national level, do not become discouraged. Many fine secular mediators are available, so you don't have to give up on mediation. Use your phone book and check under mediation services to see what is available in the secular marketplace. You may also contact the Academy of Family Mediators, PO Box 10501, Eugene, OR 97440, 503/345-1205, for referrals.

Bibliography

Ahrons, C. R. and Rodgers, R. H. *Divorced Families.* New York: W. W. Norton & Company, 1987.

Bienfield, Florence. *My Mom and Dad Are Getting a Divorce.* St. Paul, MN: EMC Corporation, 1978.

Blades, Joan. *Mediate Your Divorce, A Guide to Cooperative Custody, Property and Support Agreements.* Englewood Cliffs, N.J.: Prentice Hall, 1985.

Coogler, O. J. *Structured Mediation in Divorce Settlement: A Hanbook for Marital Mediation.* Lexington, Mass.: Lexington Books, 1978.

Dingwall, Robert, and Eekelaar, John. *Divorce, Mediation and the Legal Process.* Oxford: Clarendon Press, 1988.

Divorce Mediation: Theory and Practice. Eds. Jay Folberg and Ann Milne. New York: Guilford Press, 1988.

Erickson, Stephen K., and Erickson, Marilyn S. McKnight. *Family Mediation Casebook, Theory and Process.* New York: Brunner/Mazel Publishers, 1989.

Family Law Section, American Bar Association, *Standards of Practice for Mediators,* Chicago, Ill.

Folberg, J., and Taylor, A. *Mediation: A Comprehensive Guide to Resolving Disputes without Litigation.* San Francisco: Jossey Bass, 1981. Revised 4/1989.

Hanson, Freya O., "Mediating Marriage Muddles," *The Lutheran,* April 1, 1987.

Neumann, Diane. *Divorce Mediation: How to Cut the Cost and Stress of Divorce.* Orlando: Holt, Rinehart & Winston, Inc., 1989.

Pleasant, Emanuel, "Mediation for Reconciliation," *Mediation Quarterly, Journal of the Academy of Family Mediators,* Number 21, Fall, 1988.

Ricci, Isolina. *Mom's House, Dad's House: Making Shared Custody Work.* New York: MacMillan, 1980.

Schneider & Schneider. *Divorce Mediation.* Washington, D. C.: Acropolis Books Ltd., 1984.

Ury, William and Roger Fisher. *Getting to Yes: Negotiating Agreement Without Giving In.* New York: Houghton-Mifflin, 1981.

Vermont Law School. *The Role of Mediation in Divorce Proceedings: A Comparative Perspective.* Dispute Resolution Project. South Royalton, Vermont, 1987.

Wallerstein, Judith and Kelly, Joan. *Surviving the Breakup: How Children and Parents Cope with Divorce.* New York: Basic Books, 1980.

Wallerstein, Judith S. and Blakeslee, Sandra. *Second Chances: Men, Women & Children a Decade After Divorce. Who Wins, Who Loses—and Why.* New York: Ticknor & Fields, 1989.

This bibliography is not intended to be comprehensive, but is simply given for its practical value. Please note that none of these books specifically addresses the issue of divorce mediation as a church sanctioned program.